SESSION MATTERS
A Book for Elders

Stewart Matthew

THE SAINT ANDREW PRESS

EDINBURGH

First published in 1990 by
THE SAINT ANDREW PRESS
121 George Street, Edinburgh EH2 4YN

Copyright © Stewart G Matthew 1990

ISBN 0 7152 0644 3

British Library Cataloguing in Publication Data
Matthew, Stewart
     Session Matters.
     1. Church of Scotland. Elders. Duties
     I. Title
     262.15

ISBN 0-7152-0644-3

This book has been set in 10/12 pt Palatino

Printed and bound by Bell and Bain Ltd., Glasgow

CONTENTS

FOREWORD
Ronald Barclay

It has been said, 'Jesus taught the adults and played with the children; His Church teaches the children and plays with the adults'. The concept of Adult Christian Education has been a problem to the Church for many years and it is only recently that new approaches and determined efforts by some people have brought about changes in what was an unsatisfactory situation. The remarkable increase in interest in elder training is an example of this trend. Stewart Matthew has done more than any other person to encourage elders and lay people, along with ministers, to become involved in this shared ministry and leadership team. This book is a collection of helpful and supportive comments which have appeared in *Life and Work* in the 'Session Matters' column over the years and which have been of great assistance to those people searching for answers to the question 'what can I do?'

Starting from the assertion that any elder is *not* better that no elder at all, Stewart Matthew leads us through important topics such as the idea of a contract for elders; positive and enabling leadership; training; pastoral topics (such as bereavement, caring, how often should we visit and how long should each visit last, praying in our districts, and so on); the flexibility principle; elder burn-out and sabbatical leave for elders. With inherent good sense and a clear sense of purpose the author brings help, encouragement and practical advice to his readers and makes a vigorous attempt to help people answer the question 'what can I do?' If you believe that 'the laymen are not there to help the minister run the church; the minister is there to help the laymen *be* the church,' this book will challenge and stimulate you. If you are not sure about becoming an enabler, a leader of the team, a member of the shared ministry, this book will give you the information you need to make your decision. This is, indeed, a book which brings us all together, in our service as lay-people and ministers, to lead and to care for God's people.

April 1990

ABOUT THE AUTHOR

In 1969, following a period working as a teacher of religious education in England, Stewart Matthew returned to Scotland to be the parish minister of St Ninian's Bellfield in Kilmarnock. One of the features of his ministry there was the development of a session which understood the *shared ministry* of all God's people and which provided positive leadership to its congregation. Teamwork in Christ was an essential factor.

In 1979 Stewart joined the staff of the Church of Scotland's Department of Education, from which base he has tried to encourage sessions to see themselves as the ordained leadership teams of their congregations. He has developed a wide range of learning materials and training opportunities for elders throughout Scotland and has worked with other presbyterian denominations in this regard. Within the Church of Scotland he has forged links between those involved in the education and training of elders and those involved in encouraging a missionary spirit.

'Session Matters' first appeared in the columns of *Life and Work*, the Church of Scotland's monthly magazine. They are reproduced by kind permission of Mr R D Kernohan, Editor of *Life and Work*.

PREFACE

The following extract comes from the congregational magazine of the congregation I grew up in as a boy. Though not the minister of the congregation, my father was the editor of the magazine. In due course he was ordained as an elder. The extract, edited by my father, contains what at ordination after ordination elders were told back in the 50s and 60s.

'THERE IS NOTHING MORE SACRED YOU WILL BE CALLED UPON TO DO THAN TO BE THE ROYAL CUP-BEARER FOR CHRIST.'

What it means to be an Elder

WE CALL NURSING a vocation. An electrician has a job; a nurse has a vocation, but it is not meant in any sense to be a snobbish term. A job can be exalted into a vocation when people throw in their heart, their mind and their soul in utter devotion to their particular sort of service. Then any job becomes a vocation. When we use the word vocation, it means a person's heart is in it.

The Eldership, gentlemen, is a vocation, therefore it has the same implication. You shall put your whole heart into it. *I doubtless told some of you that the duties of the Eldership were light. They are not burdensome.* They are light if you regard them purely as the fulfilment or discharge of a duty.

It is the way that you do it that counts. If you have your heart in it, then let us talk no more about the duties of an Elder, but let us rather say the vocation of an Elder.

The Three Tasks

The Doorman

The first duty is a very simple one. The Elder stands at the door to welcome the people as they approach the Church. A simple task. In fact, it is so simple that at times it might tend to be neglected.

The Church is the human attempt to create a heavenly atmosphere on earth, and a person comes to the door of the House of God as a person comes to the door of any house. They will not in this case expect their Host to be there to welcome them. You will not find Christ at the door, but you will find an Elder doing his door duty. If that Elder regards it as a vocation, don't you see what is going to happen? In his welcome, whether it be smile or spoken word, he is going to help those who come to sense that this is the House of God, as though Christ Himself were standing at the door!

The Elder who regards his duty at the door as a vocation may not be aware of it, but he is conveying to the people who come in, before they come inside these walls, the conception that this is truly the House of God. You are no less than the representative of Christ Himself. As you stand at the door, gentlemen, you are bearing the welcome of Christ!

The Spiritual Postman

You will have a district to go round before Communion. In that sense you are a sort of spiritual postman. Isn't our mail called the Royal Mail? And is not every postman a Royal official? So is the Elder. The Elder is the Royal messenger bearing the invitation of our Master to His banquet. If it is regarded just as a duty, then the prime thing obviously is that the Elder has in his hand a bundle of cards for a certain number of people. These are the people who were at Communion last time. There may be one or two new ones, and his main job is to get rid of those cards and deliver them to the members concerned. If the Elder regards his visitation as having real meaning, if his heart is in it, what is he going to say to himself? I am the bearer of a Royal invitation, but I have no card for this particular house. What shall I do? Shall I pass this house by? Shall I, therefore, withhold from that house the Royal invitation? He will certainly not do that.

What is a Communion card but a mute scrap of paper? When the Elder visits in person, speaks to the people, hands the card over, the whole influence of his visit can add something to the mute invitation. The Elder finds himself in his district the bearer of the Royal invitation to the Lord's Supper.

The Royal Cup-Bearer

Of course, *his most sacred task will really be at Communion*. Here again we use the familiar term, 'Communion duties'. This is concerned with the purely mechanical process of dispensing Communion to a large congregation. If an Elder regards this in any sense as a vocation, then surely he sees what it involves. What is the Elder doing? Between this Table and all these pews on the Communion occasion stands an Elder. The Elder lifts the Cup of Salvation and he carries it from this Table and hands it round the pews. The Elder is the Royal Cup-Bearer. Surely that is the most sacred thing of all. There are occasions in life when you have a success, when you will be congratulated, when you do something noteworthy, render a great service to others. There are occasions in life which stand out as red letter days in your memory. Over and above every experience of life, gentlemen, I say this to you. There is nothing more sacred that you will ever be called to do than to be the Royal Cup-Bearer for Christ at His banquet.

I gave you a text because it had in it the word vocation. I tried to say to you your Eldership is a vocation. Now I give you another text, and of the two this one has pride of place. It comes from the Book of Nehemiah, chapter 1 verse 11—'I was the King's Cup-Bearer'. Gentlemen, today you become the King's Cup-Bearers. As you stand at the door, and become the bearer of the King's welcome, you are the bearer of Christ's welcome. As you visit your fellow-members, you are the bearer of Christ's welcome. As you play your part at Communion, you are the bearer of Christ's Cup of Salvation. Is not all that a great and wondrous vocation which demands your heart, your mind, your soul in the discharge of all you are asked to do?

My Father enthusiastically edited that sad piece of teaching. He was to come to know better. I confess to having been responsible for the italics and the two sub-headings—'The Doorman' and 'The Spiritual Postman'.

I remember all of this being given again and again with considerable oratorical skill. Even as a teenager I knew that little was being said loudly. The stumbling efforts of the Church of Scotland's Panel on Doctrine regarding the Eldership throughout the 1980s have owed much to this trivialising of the Eldership.

When I was licensed to preach, and invited to do so from my local pulpit, I pointed out that the three tasks mentioned in the ordination address could be carried out by the boys of the Boy's Brigade. It was an immature form of suicide, ensuring that I never again preached in that pulpit.

I was first introduced to the potential of the Presbyterian eldership when I served as an assistant minister in St Columba's, Glenrothes. I began to see that what I had heard over and over again as a boy was not just a little spoken loudly, but a serious trivialising of the eldership. My father encouraged me to write for his magazine. In February 1966 the following was published.

Writing Home to Nazareth
by Revd Stewart G Matthew, BD

THIS IS THE second of my letters to you about the parish of St Columba's in Glenrothes, where I am at present Assistant Minister. St Columba's is, in my opinion, despite its modern building, a traditional congregation, but one which is making the Church and the Parish system relevant in modern society. In this the Eldership has an extremely important part to play.

So often the role of an Elder has degenerated into three tasks, namely, the delivering of Communion cards, often, sadly, via the letter box: standing at the church doors to welcome the congregation: distributing the elements at the Lord's Supper. I would not like to see these tasks taken from the Elder, but the fact is that in the Church of Scotland these three duties can be done by anyone in the congregation. The members of the Youth Fellowship could do them. The role of an Elder is far more dynamic and meaningful than this! It is a heavy job with great responsibilities, not one to be given to a 'respectable' business man in the hope that he will thereafter come more regularly to church! In the town of St Andrews I met one such business man who had been invited to join a Kirk Session. He rarely went to a service and had far more respect for the Eldership than the Kirk Session which issued the invitation. He declined the offer. In St Columba's, the Elder is a key figure. He is expected to devote an evening a week to his parish work. How he could hope to do it on less escapes me. An Elder has the pastoral oversight of his district. He must know his people, be able to discuss their problems, encourage them to commit their time and talents to the work of the congregation.

An important feature of St Columba's is the District Gathering. Once a month the Elder of a district (sometimes they work in pairs) invites all the members of the district to a gathering in one of the homes. At this meeting they study the Scriptures or some book which helps them to develop a more knowledgeable and mature faith. The atmosphere is informal. This permits people to discuss their problems, express their doubts and be of help to each other. After the study the group move on to what is called District Care. Here they discuss in what ways they can be of service to the wider community. The District Gathering is, therefore, a means of encouraging Christian fellowship and missionary activity—the two hall-marks of the Church.

The monthly Session meeting begins always with a period of study in preparation for the District Gatherings. Each Elder, working with his Board member, organises his district, with a secretary where possible, a magazine distributor and a building fund collector. At every point in this congregation there is an effort to spread the work of the congregation, involving as many people as possible. This helps people to feel a part of the congregation. There is no Church Officer here (apologies to Mr Cook!). We look after our own second home which, by the way, is open all day, every day. Teams of people look after the maintenance of the buildings and the grounds. Not everyone is capable of being an Elder, but if God has given someone the talent of joinery or gardening, there is the opportunity in this congregation for him to use that talent.

Next month I will write about the Christian Education programme. Until then, kindest regards from Irene and myself.

It is interesting to see in this article the seeds of what was to flourish in terms of Session leadership when I became minister of St Ninian's Bellfield and to be spread further through my work for the Church of Scotland's Department of Education.

I am grateful to Robert Kernohan, the Editor of Life and Work, who from 1982 permitted me space to promote my ideas about the corporate leadership role of the Session, the importance of teamwork in the achieving of leadership goals, and the elevating of pastoral work beyond the level of a 'Spiritual postperson'.

I am grateful, too, for belonging to the Eldership Working Party which has made a useful contribution to reclaiming the Presbyterian Eldership applying to its own work what it believes applies to the Eldership.

STEWART MATTHEW
16 February 1990

The Kirk Session of St Ninian's Bellfield, 1979

TEAM MANAGEMENT

'What is there for us to do?'

THE ESTABLISHMENT of a congregational board in one congregation evoked the telling question from some elders: *'But what will there be left for us to do?'*

The business of a congregational board—the handling of the congregation's financial and property affairs—requires spiritual depth. The session is represented on the board. But the requirements of an elder are different from the requirements of a member of the

board alone *because the work of the session is so much wider.*

Most, if not all, congregational boards have at least two committees —a finance committee and a property committee—consisting of people with particular talents in these directions, be they elders or managers. Sometimes the latter may be more skilled in these matters, though they may not yet have the spiritual depth required of an elder, nor be able to devote the time that serious eldership calls for.

Few sessions, although I think the scene is changing, have such a

1

committee or sub-group structure. This is surprising when you appreciate that the session exists to develop the congregation's ability to reach out in effective missionary ways to its community; to create a fellowship life within the congregation to support and equip its members for this purpose and into which new members and enquirers can be integrated. It exists also to develop a comprehensive Christian education programme for all the members of the congregation; and to foster wider links with the Church of Scotland as a whole and with other denominations and caring agencies in the area.

It seems to me that the exercise of leadership like this requires some kind of sub-group structure to permit people who have particular talents in these directions to concentrate on these areas and bring sound proposals for the judgment of the court.

The major problem for a session with the old-fashioned constitution, even meeting monthly, would surely be to find the time to do this while also handling the important, and often time-consuming, matters of finance and fabric. Clearly, of course, the work of both bodies will continually impinge upon each other.

A similar anxiety to the one mentioned above was raised in a session which discussed the possibility of not having elders seated around the Communion Table at the celebration of the sacrament. Some feared that the session would become totally invisible to the congregation!

No devoted pastoral elder could ever become invisible, nor could the members of a session which exercises real leadership of the life of the congregation.

September 1983

"What do you mean, I don't seem very receptive to new ideas?!!!!"

The Elect

MY FORMER session had always used the method of electing elders by the vote of the session itself. Any system is open to error, but I saw no reason to seek to change this procedure. Together, however, we evolved the following decision process.

At the session meeting a month or two after the decision that it was time to make more appointments, names were suggested for prayerful consideration. This was done on the clear understanding that no discussion would take place at this stage with the people concerned. It was agreed that the election would take place at the following kirk session meeting.

On the evening of the election, session reminded itself of three things:

(1) The confidential nature of what was to take place and that any breach of confidentiality would be a matter for session discipline, because it was important that each elder should feel free to speak as he/she felt led;

(2) The importance of what we were about to do, not least for the people we might ask to consider taking the vows of eldership, which are akin to marriage vows;

(3) There being no magical required number of new elders, the people who would be nominated were in no way in competition with each other.

Shared opinion

Nominations were then called for with a brief comment to justify the nomination. A list was formed of those who received a seconder. The nominator and seconder of the first name on the list were invited to speak. Full and frank discussion followed. When the session felt ready to undertake the *first vote*, each elder was able to vote—'For the nomination', 'Against the nomination', 'Don't know whether the time is right', or 'Don't know the person'.

The 'Don't know whether the time is right' category permitted support for the nomination, but consideration for the person's present family circumstances, work situation or whatever might place too heavy a burden on the person at this point in time. The 'Don't know the person' category allowed people to escape from a 'For' vote simply because they did not wish to oppose the nomination.

The vote of the session was charted for all to see. Then came the *second vote*. Each elder voted 'Elect' or 'Not elect', not in terms of his or her view regarding the person, but in terms of his or her view regarding the strength of the session's shared opinion. Before the voting had begun, we had

3

decided that if, for example, there were 22 of us present at the meeting, then 19 'Elect' votes would be required for a person to be approached.

And so we moved slowly down the list.

The result of this was that the session was rarely able to make many approaches to people at any one time, but those whom it did approach were the people whom it really believed to have the potential to become committed and effective elders.

These election evenings I remember as being moving and fascinating experiences for all of us and had, I think, a bearing on the subsequent integration of the new elders into our team.

December 1982

How many Elders do we need?

PASTORAL WORK is an important aspect of eldership. Certainly we require enough elders for this so as not to over-burden anyone or to reduce pastoral concern to rare fleeting visits of little consequence. Some elders may be able to exercise *meaningful* pastoral concern (listening, befriending,

sharing faith) to over 20 homes. For most 15 homes may be the maximum. For others, *eg* new elders, the number may have to be less.

Does your session think along these lines or does it just fill vacancies without ever looking at the question afresh?

A number of sessions answer the question as follows. An average number of visits per elder (*eg* 15) is established and divided into the number of homes of the congregation (*eg* 450). From this figure (*eg* 30) is subtracted the present strength of the session (*eg* 24) and the figure of elders required (*eg* 6) is arrived at.

Team Strategy

This procedure overlooks the fact that an elder is called to have a parish concern, not just a membership concern. However, if these *six* people are found by good procedures (the subject of an earlier column) at least one part of our responsibility is covered. But what if they cannot be found?

In my former session we devised together a *team eldership*. The parish was divided into eight areas and a team of three or four elders established in each area. This strategy, which is being worked

by some sessions, can be very effective, permitting flexibility in a number of directions which the one person/one district strategy precludes. Each team had its allocation of managers and the support of those who took part in the monthly house church. The elders supervised the pastoral concern, indeed did most of it, but had the help of others where and when needed. For example, where there were rows of senior citizens' homes, where opening the door at night was not particularly liked, other people's talents and skills were employed during the day (and often more frequently than the elder could manage).

But even if the *six* can be found, the question has not been adequately answered. How many elders should we have? Sufficient for the job. What is the job? The provision of real leadership to the congregation—a much wider

matter than pastoral concern for members.

If we place the emphasis on leadership we may want to ordain people without giving them a district to tend because we want their leadership and spiritual expertise and skills to be present at our session meetings. It may be that they give this commitment, and what it leads them into, but are not able to include meaningful district work in their busy schedules. It may be that they do not have the ability to do district work.

Is it possible to give a definitive answer to the question put to me? I don't think so. We certainly have to resist working on an 'any elder is better than no elder' principle, which becomes even more crucial for an unthinking session that provides no adequate preparation of those it invites into its ranks and no in-service training.

March 1983

Contract—or just a wee chat?

WHAT KIND of preparation programme were you given for your decision 'yes' or 'no' to the call to the eldership? What kind of contract, written or implied, did you enter into?

The situation is changing, but many elders admit to little more than what they call 'a chat with the minister'. Many of them I think feel cheated by this.

This may also explain in part the kind of comment—'I've been an elder for years. I don't need any training'. This may cloak fear. It may simply reveal ignorance. It is certainly a great discouragement to many of the new elders.

Elders who came in on an unwritten contract and with little preparation, with the implication that there is little more to the role of an elder than some basic duties and routine church maintenance —despite the considerable oratory in which the little may have been couched—need our special attention.

Good question

As more and more elders and sessions are developing their work, wanting to play in a higher league, requiring more of their team, it has become apparent to me that we have to take care of those who came in on a light-weight contract. It is not fair, let alone loving and productive, to point an accusing, parental finger at them. They did not contract to play in a higher league. They therefore require and deserve the opportunity, however it is done, to re-contract—to contract *in* to the new expectations, or to contract *out* and with dignity.

At a very basic training programme in one Presbytery, an elder at the end of the course said—'This training is good. Why wasn't I given this before becoming an elder?' I agreed that that was a good question, but, having established that he had been an elder for a number of years, during which time his session had appointed other elders, I asked—'What kind of preparation did *you* give *them*?'

Now that you are an elder and

part of the vitally important selection process, what do you and your fellow-elders offer by way of preparation and clear contract? If it is little or nothing —'a chat with the minister'—the responsibility, or irresponsibility, is a shared thing.

February 1987

When new blood comes in

BEFORE GOING to my first charge I had read everything I could lay my hands on about the previous life of the congregation. Continuity is important. I remember, however, making a silly mistake. Indeed I remember making many silly mistakes. This particular one related to the congregational magazine.

A new editor was required and, being interested in church journalism, I assumed the task. I began a new look, new format magazine and, while retaining the same title for the magazine, brought out my first edition as volume 1, number 1!

Because the new minister did not live the congregation's past, it can be, for him or her, as if it had never existed. A new elder can fall into the same trap.

We owe the past much, but we can need help to understand it and so be helped to understand the present and to move forward effectively.

It is too idealistic to believe that a session should be willing and able to explain to its new minister—or new ruling elders —what, as the leadership team of the congregation, it has been trying to achieve in the years prior to their arrival? Should it not be able to articulate its strengths and weaknesses, its hopes and dreams for the future?

Should the session not also be open to the new members' hopes and dreams; to their understanding of the purpose of a congregation and the nature of its shared ministry, including the role of the session (which includes the minister)? 'We never did it that way before . . .' can be a right enthusiasm crusher.

As the prophet said: 'Where there is no vision the people perish'.

A session requires times of reassessment, when it asks itself some very basic questions about its work. Experience, it is often said, is our teacher. But it is not that simple. Without reassessment, the same mistake may be perpetrated for years and the same blind points go unnoticed.

An annual stewardship theme is a useful policy to have. By stewardship I don't just mean the financial aspect of the congregation, but rather the whole life-style of the congregation. The theme can be the response to the basic question—'What is God calling *us* to concentrate on in particular in our part of His vineyard?' I wonder how many sessions regularly pause along the way to ask such a question to enable it to move forward.

Someone once wrote: 'We are pilgrims, travellers, adventurers and all the while we must be travelling on.'

November 1982

Playing as a team

THREE FAIR-SIZED steps were all that were required to take us from the front door of our church plant, out of the often wet Kilmarnock weather, across the narrow vestibule area to the door of the worship area.

Once through that door there was nowhere to go but into one of the rows of fixed pews, to gaze at the back of the heads of those who were sitting in the pews further forward.

To provide a better meeting and reception area, some of us had the idea of removing some of the back pews. The idea was not popular with some elders. I understand traditional ideas and reserve about rearranging the 'house of God'.

The matter was not pressed but it kept coming up. After about a year it came up yet again, and an elder who was not in favour of the change said, to my mind, much to his credit—'Moderator, it is clear that some of us do not want this to be done. It is also clear that most of the session do want this to be done. Take the pews out.'

The following Sunday I announced that those who liked the back pews would still find them next Sunday, but they would be five rows further forward. And it was so!

It can be a terrible thing to do to Presbyterians, to move the back pews, but it hardly caused a ripple in the congregation. Why? Because not one elder, to my knowledge, said, outside session, 'But I told them not to do it'. We had learned to play by the rule of Capital 'T' over little 'i'.

Loyalty to the team had become more important than individual points of view. That is not to say that individual points of view should not be held, worked for and indeed, if felt necessary in matters of serious principle, resigned over.

It is to suggest that once session has come to a decision, that decision is to be collectively upheld by all who remain on the session.

April 1988

Ordination

Does an elder's ordination mean the same thing as a minister's, although to a different office?

THE ANSWER is 'yes'. Ordination has to do with Church order. It is the setting apart of a person to a particular office of particular importance and responsibility in the Church's decision-making

procedures. Ordination has therefore to do with authorisation —and to do with recognition on the part of the Church that the person ordained has been called by God to a special ministry, within the ministry of the whole Church. In both cases ordination is for life, hence re-ordination does not take place. Sometimes people question this, at least in regard to the 'ruling' elders. I think of vows of ordination as being like marriage vows. Divorce may be possible, perhaps sometimes sadly necessary, but not what is intended. The intention is a life-long vocation.

March 1983

In the Chair

Do we always need a minister to chair session meetings?

MINISTERS NEED not chair the congregational board. I certainly found it better not to do so. The session, however, is a different matter. Unlike the board, the session is a court of the Church of Scotland. It is the body called to head and direct the whole lifestyle of a congregation and, according to our practice, it has to

9

be chaired by the minister. He is subject to the superior courts but, unlike the other members of the session, is not subject to the session. In a vacancy, the Presbytery appoints a minister to act as interim-moderator.

I understand that in an enforced absence a minister may give written authority to another minister to hold and chair a meeting of the session for a specific purpose. In a crisis, for example the minister being rushed into hospital half an hour before the session meeting, an informal meeting can be held, but any decisions taken would have to be confirmed (homologated) at a subsequent, and properly constituted, session meeting.

In my opinion, the important role of the minister today is positive (and enabling) leadership. I have some difficulty with the strict concept of the minister as 'moderator', though I would wish to maintain that he/she is an elder among elders. However, the more skilled the leadership, the more enabling of others it becomes, the more the minister will moderate between the creative views of a session that employs good management procedures and is alive to the issues of Christian leadership.

Although a minister has to chair the session, he/she may need help to develop good management procedures. A degree in theology does not represent a good qualification in management skills!

May 1983

LEARN TO DELEGATE

Beware of stars?

I HAVE childhood memories of the football star, Billy Steel. Billy could start the ball 'way down Dens Road in Dundee. He could work the ball through everyone on the pavement, make his way into Dens Park, pass all his own team, beat all the opposition and score a goal! He had flair. He was a star.

People with flair, star quality, can be very useful in a team but, as the elders of Campbeltown told me one Friday evening, we must 'beware stars'. Their comment has

10

stuck with me. They were so right. A star is not a team and a team is not a star.

As elders we must 'beware stars' for at least two reasons. It always heartens me when, at work with a session, I hear the talents of the minister appreciated. But *star dependency* must be guarded against. For one reason, too much can be expected of the star.

'We used to have a youth fellowship. It's about time the new minister got one going again.'

'We need more people joining the congregation. What's the minister doing about *that*?'

'The old folks are needing more attention. The minister should be doing more visiting.'

Beware stars!

Collective role

The other reason can be seen in the life of a congregation, which is only good at what the present minister is good at and interested in. When a new minister comes along it is all change, and the congregation becomes good at what the new 'star' is good at, and no longer at what the former minister was good at.

Ministers come and go, hopefully bringing flair and expertise. Sessions are on-going. It is the eldership team which is the guardian of the tradition of the congregation. It is up to the session to ensure that skills are learned and accumulated by the session and by the congregation.

And one last point. Ministers and sessions must not domesticate the membership. Their collective role is to release the potential of the members to 'play' as well as they can.

March 1987

Two questions of moderation

AS I BEGAN to write this column we were approaching a General Election. Any political party which had some 50,000 leaders (many of them full time workers for the party), in some 1500 committed party machines in a great national network, would almost certainly win!

I'm not suggesting that we should seek as the Church to become the Government of the land, but I am pointing to the potential the Church of Scotland has for making a Christian impact upon our society.

That we do make an enormous contribution to the life of our

11

nation is beyond dispute. That we are not realising our full potential is also, I think, beyond dispute.

Last year my daughter returned from Camus, the Iona Community's junior youth camp, with the question: 'Dad, what does the local session have to say about the bomb?' Well, what does *your* session have to say about the nuclear issue? Is such a matter on the session agenda? More importantly, what are our sessions doing about peace-making? It is easy to deplore a situation. Anyone can do that. Christians are called to be constructive, creative.

My daughter might also have asked about what the session is saying and doing about the job she feels will not be there for her, even if she passes her exams.

Recently I asked a group of elders to list the issues they considered to be of most consequence in today's society. Their list included the nuclear issue, work and unemployment, family life (generation gap, marriage breakdown), drug abuse, the Third World, and use of natural resources. When asked how these crucial issues were being expressed in the life-styles of their congregations, they admitted, with one or two notable exceptions, that these topics were not on the agenda!

There was no room for Jesus in the inn. How much room do we give him, and the things he calls us to be interested in and involved in, on our session agendas?

When talking to elders about such matters, or about the development of adult Christian education in their congregation, or perhaps about the development of house groups at the heart of the life of the congregation, one senses the fear they have of the opposition and apathy they may have to face in the implementation of such matters.

In the session the minister is known as the 'Moderator'. It is an interesting title. I take it to mean that the minister is meant in the session to moderate between the creative views of his/her fellow-elders. The task is to harness the creativity, not in the sense of restricting it, but in the sense of encouraging it, gathering it together and enabling it to find practical expression.

With all the collective talents and experience present in a session, attuned to the adventurous Spirit of God who is always out in front of us, as well as journeying with us, creativity should abound in our kirk sessions. No moderator should be able to restrict this creativity, including those who seek to reverse the roles and to 'moderate' (restrict, crush) the enthusiasms and creativity of their minister or fellow-elders.

July 1982

A 'transference' problem

THINK OF A GROUP of children being taught about road safety. It's the last hour of the school day, but the children are enjoying the lesson. Street diagrams, photographs, slides, video cassettes are all being used to help them understand the dangers and how to take care of themselves. A policeman is there to impress the importance of the topic on them and to check out their understanding. Clearly they understand. The bell rings and off the children go, straight across the road outside the school, without looking to right or left!

What they learned in the one situation (the classroom) they did not transfer and apply to the other situation (the street). It seems to me that many sessions make the same mistake in a quite crucial area.

Many sessions—especially those who have been helped, by their minister or whoever, to escape the domestication of the concept, of *'the* minister'—readily agree that the session is the leadership team of the congregation. Having asked hundreds of elders to work out the essentials of good, effective teamwork, I know that Kirk elders know a lot about the teamwork.

They know about the importance of understanding the game, good team selection procedures, skills development, position-playing, mutual support and understanding, confidence building, *etc, etc*. A lot of this knowledge is not, however, being transferred to the life of sessions and being applied to how they spend their time and carry out their work.

Take, for example, training. Every group of elders tells me that training is obviously an essential of effective teamwork. When I ask them to outline their session's training programme, there is often a silence, sharply highlighting this problem of transference.

There are two essentials of effective teamwork which are rarely transferred and applied by sessions because they are often just not thought about. While appreciated in sport and commerce, they are often overlooked in many

13

important spheres of life. I refer to assessment and forward planning, which are, of course, closely related.

Both have a personal importance for each of us as we ask: How well am I doing my work? What help do I need? How am I using my time? What changes could I usefully make?

Both have a team importance. What have we achieved in the past year? What has helped or hindered our progress? What do we need to concentrate more upon?

As sessions we certainly need to spend time assessing the effectiveness of our teamwork and the quality of our leadership of the congregation. We need to consider where, as God's people, our shared ministry has got to, and what areas of activity God may wish us to discontinue or begin.

November 1987

Training in Eldership

'THERE IS a great sense of relief in talking to someone who is in the same position as oneself!' So began a report I received from Mrs Helen Russell, the then energetic education convener of Abernethy Presbytery.

She continued: 'Seventy elders of the Presbytery found this relief and encouragement when they met together for a day conference in February. That so many had come, approximately 50 per cent of all the elders of the Presbytery, shows how real is the need. Speakers were followed by discussion in small groups: listening to the groups it was clear that the elders wanted to talk about their work and the challenge it entailed.

'There was a feeling that not enough was being asked of them. Some had even been told— "there's not much to it." There was a sense of frustration that their ordination had promised something which had never been fulfilled. Many had had little or no training, nor had there been refresher courses. The opportunities offered by this conference were therefore much appreciated.'

I was delighted to receive that report. I hope that some of the elders who attended might join with Helen in the development of further opportunities for training in their Presbytery.

In Edinburgh Presbytery there is a group of elders who took part in Edinburgh's 1982 eldership training programme, and who have helped to prepare this year's programme which has offered a choice of three five-week courses —a basic course on 'Approaching Ordination to the Eldership', a course on developing adult education in the congregation, and a pastoral course entitled 'Beyond the Doorstep'—the title of a similar course which is being offered in Glasgow Presbytery.

The Kirk's Education Department, in conjunction with the Home Mission Department, sent out some months ago a leaflet to every elder in the Kirk about training and the resources available. It is also trying to encourage an annual training in eldership programme in every Presbytery. Do elders merit less than this?

The session has to be a priority in our form of Church government. It is the door, open or shut, to new life in our congregations.

June 1983

'Why weren't we told?'

I REMEMBER on one occasion being told very forcibly by a group of elders—'That's the trouble with you 121 people. You don't tell us what is available'. Often I meet people who express, more gently (!), their regret about not knowing about a course they would have taken part in, had they but known about it.

One of the problems within the Church is the problem of communication, for example making sure ministers, elders, and others are made aware of the resource materials and opportunities available to them. Because of logistical factors and financial restrictions, most of the communications relating to congregational life go through the general mailing—the monthly mailing from the central offices to all ministers and other key people.

A typical monthly mailing may include material relating to a 'special season' (Education, Ministry and Mission, World Mission and Unity, Social Responsibility). It is likely to include information about courses and resources for working with, for example, elders, parents, children, the bereaved, the community at large. It may contain items on church finance, heating and lighting, other church property matters, and so on. The monthly mailing contains a lot of useful items, relevant to the active life of a congregation.

Many ministers make good use of the material, or at least as much of it as they can. Others file it away

15

"DO WE NEED A VOTE TO ALTER GOD'S WILL?"

carefully, hoping to get round to it at a later date when time permits. Often *later* never comes. Others complain and talk about how they consign it all to 'the bucket'.

I find this latter course of action sad, though, having served as a parish minister, I have some understanding of why the communication doesn't get through. Ministers have a heavy workload. The monthly mailing can be viewed as a burden. For some it may be an emotional burden. This can be very true of the conscientious minister who is trying very hard to cope with the wide remit of a parish minister. The monthly mailing, with all its opportunities, can remind such ministers of areas of work which they would

like to tackle if only they could find enough hours in the week to do so. They can choose to feel guilty about this.

As well as a possible emotional problem, what we have here is a management problem—one which elders could discuss with their minister. Some items in the monthly mailing the minister should deal with, and will want to deal with, personally. Other items could be passed on to other people in the congregation. The session clerk, or one of the elders, could, for example, be responsible for the information about resources for elders, and for ensuring that his or her fellow-elders are told about these resources and encouraged to make use of them.

March 1988

CONGREGATIONAL LIFE-STYLE

Generating enthusiasm

HAVE YOU seen the rainbow posters with the message 'There is hope'? Every time I see one, I am grateful to whoever brought them into being. If I'm feeling down or harassed, they provide a good reminder. Our jaded society of so many broken relationships and lost enthusiasms needs their message.

I heard about a lady whose life was so empty that each day she woke up with the hopeless thought—'Dear God, morning'. No doubt she would have echoed Scrooge's 'Humbug' reply to the greeting 'Merry Christmas'. Her life, like his, was boring, pointless, empty—devoid of enthusiasm.

Christmas is, of course, not humbug. It is the priceless offer, in Jesus, of life, energy and more than hope, enthusiasm.

Scrooge's life, and perhaps the lady's, lacked good relationships.

Happily Scrooge in the story rediscovered relationships and enthusiasm. A Christian friend helped the lady to find new enthusiasm. Her waking thought became the genuine prayer— 'Good Morning, God'.

Our society needs congregations that offer hope and encourage enthusiasm. The congregations which do this best are probably the ones which concentrate on building relationships—developing real warmth and love between the members, and between their members and those outwith the Christian family.

In our tradition the doing of this hinges very much upon the leadership we elders provide, the enthusiasm we generate. Christmas is a good time for us in our sessions to consider taking agenda time to reflect together on the ways we encourage, or *could* encourage, our members and the non-Christians in the society around us, to awake with the genuine prayer—'Good Morning, God'.

December 1986

Not uncaring—just careless

LAST YEAR my wife and I were given a wedding anniversary present by our daughter—two tickets for an Everly Brothers reunion concert. That dates us, as it did the rest of the audience! As we entered the auditorium, having had our tickets cut in two by a disinterested person, the usherette looked at us and let us pass by to search for our seats unaided. It was a cold welcome to the theatre.

We enjoyed the show. No doubt the theatre owners and staff, and Don and Phil Everly, were glad we were there, to receive our ticket money, but we came and went with no attention paid to us. No one knew we were there—and no one really cared about us.

Entering a sanctuary to join in the worship of God should be a very different experience. With all that our faith teaches us about God's love, Christian togetherness, concern for the stranger, one would expect a real warmth of welcome. Even if the minister bids all welcome from the pulpit, it is important that members of the congregation somehow express their joy in sharing this time of worship together.

As elders we should be encouraging this.

For many years I had the pulpit to pew view. The pew to pulpit view can be a very different one. Like ministers, office-bearers have their place, their status, their Sunday duties. We are 'at home', but we can be blind to those who don't have our involvement. The stranger or fringe-member—perhaps someone seeking to find the way 'home'—can be overlooked. We don't mean to be uncaring, but we can be careless.

When on door-duty I trust we are never like that usherette, but we can get engrossed in conversation with our fellow office-bearers, enjoying each other's company, transacting church business, and the stranger can pass by with barely a glance, or with a brief 'Good Morning'.

After a warm welcome at the door, it would be good to have an elder in the sanctuary to reinforce the welcome and to offer help, if it seems appropriate, to find a pew, and perhaps someone with whom - to share the fellowship hour of worship.

We would not wish to force ourselves on anyone, but people should not be able to come and go with no real attention paid to them, feeling that no one knew that they were there and no one really cared.

June 1985

'How can we get people involved?'

I AM often asked this question by elders. The question usually applies, not to those who do not belong to the Church, but to those who do! I share keenly the sense of frustration and disappointment.

As a young minister in training, and somewhat disenchanted with the institutional Church I was experiencing, I thrilled to the idea of the ministry of all God's people—our shared ministry to each other in our congregations, and our ministry together to the world. I understood then, and still believe today, that the function of a minister has to do with encouraging and enabling the ministry of others. I feel disappointed that more progress has not been made in the involving of more of our members in a real shared ministry.

The long tradition of calling a tiny minority of God's people 'the ministers' has not helped. Some ministers who have tried to break the mould have been defeated by members who view 'ministry' as the job of 'the minister'. Progress has also been blocked by ministers who in fact view 'ministry' as, first and foremost, their job. We will all know congregations which have been de-skilled by authoritarian or parental ministers who fear, or just do not understand, the role of enabling the ministry of others. When this is allowed to happen, the session has much to answer for, though I know it can be difficult for them.

A one-sentence answer to the question about how to get people involved is, of course, not possible. There are lots of things to be looked at. One of them is, however, the kind of leadership that is being provided.

Is it authoritarian, parental (in the bad sense), domesticating, or is it encouraging, entrusting and enabling?

Is it developing a congregational life-style which has a whole range of worthwhile things going on—things which capture the heart and imagination, and harvest the great variety of interests and skills of the members?

Is it showing people that they are cared for and listened to—that their feelings and thoughts matter?

Is it supporting those who are involved and helping them to gain satisfaction from their efforts?

In our Church tradition the provision of leadership is the responsibility, not only of the minister, but of the session (which includes the minister). A session which provides, and itself models, enabling leadership will be less likely to have to ask the question.

December 1987

Annual disappointment?

IS YOUR annual congregational meeting an annual disappointment, with very few members turning out for it? Have you laid on entertainment, presentations on the work of the Church, refreshments—but with little success? Does the annual appeal for support go unheeded?

No doubt it can be argued that our members should be interested in supporting the leaders of the various congregational activities, and that they should be interested and involved in approving the financial affairs of their congregation. But clearly in many congregations they are not.

We may just accept the situation. Often we lament it. Perhaps we would do well to ask: Is it really surprising? Does an annual meeting with the emphasis on passive listening, with the invitation to ask a question which very few people will be able to take up, provide sufficient motivation?

In the past two years I have become involved in the United Reformed Church's attempts to follow the Church of Scotland's lead in developing an emphasis on what we call 'Training in Elder-ship'. I have been interested in the role of the church meeting in the URC set-up. The church meeting, open to all members, is held regul-arly, even monthly or bi-monthly. At these meetings congregation policy is worked out, and so the members feel they have more say in what goes on. They have more involvement. They are given more responsibility. The church meeting in fact appoints those it wants as its elders and lets them know what it wants of them.

While I recognise that this structure may be easier to adopt in the URC, which tends to have smaller congregations than we do, it does raise for me the question of how we communicate with *our* members. How does your session communicate with the members it leads? Do you *tell* your members what is needed, especially when the need is for money? Do you *share* with them your interests and plans and difficulties? Do you make a real effort to *listen* to your members and then feed their thoughts into your decision-making process? Do you in fact have a policy of consultation? If not, it is not surprising that few feel motivated to attend the annual meeting.

I draw your attention to the words of the late Norman Swan: 'We who sit in the pews are not to be regarded as amiable peasants, uninterested in Christian plans and with little to offer! . . . . Little or no consultation is offensive, wasteful and expensive'.

June 1987

Visiting the organisations

SINCE MOST sessions have some procedure for visiting the organis-ations of their congregations, you will probably be able to tackle the following questions:

(1) Can you remember the last such visit you made?

(2) What was the purpose of your visit?

(3) What kind of report did you give to your session?

(4) What difference did your visit make and did anything come about as a result?

If the purpose of such a visit is seen as being to bring the greetings of the session to the organisation concerned, then you, or any other elder with a cheerful disposition, could do this and simply report diligence in carrying out what was probably the annual visit.

Such a visit has the value of

B

letting the organisation know that the session has some measure of care for it.

If the procedure has more depth to it, *eg* to spot the needs of the organisations and to consider how the session could be of assistance, then it might require more than one visit per annum and that the visits be made by elders who have some knowledge about the running of the organisation and its purpose in the life of the congregation.

Supervision

This becomes even more necessary if the procedure is to include, as I think it should, supervision and assessment of the achievement of the organisation.

I heard about a minister who, early in his ministry, visited the Sunday school. This led him to give the children an examination on what they were learning. The results, being in his judgment so poor, led to the abolition of that Sunday school and the creation of a different kind of learning environment for the children.

In another congregation, one organisation had departed so far from its purpose and constitution that the session required the submission of its proposed syllabus for approval prior to printing.

We might consider these steps somewhat radical, but they did take the matter of supervision seriously.

In yet another congregation, the Sunday school superintendent was asked to speak to the session about the Sunday school.

After his report and the ensuing discussion, he was thanked for the report and for his work. He responded by saying that he had had a few sleepless nights because he had thought he was 'on the carpet'!

It had not crossed his mind that the session was simply demonstrating its genuine concern. It was the first time that the session had done so—but it was appreciated.

March 1989

More than decorative

SOME years ago a friend of mine spent some time in Zambia. His visit there was written up in *Life and Work*. In the article he recalled speaking to a Zambian elder about the extension to the elder's house —a very simple construction compared with what the work conjures up for us.

My friend learned that this

rough construction had been put up to house a weekly Bible study meeting. He learned that there were 20 elders in the area, each of whom had 100 people involved in a weekly engagement with the Bible, under the leadership of elders.

Under the auspices of our World Mission and Unity Department, Christians from different parts of the world are brought over to visit Scotland. Writing in *Life and Work* in 1985, one of them said that 'the role of elders in the Church of Scotland seems to be very limited.'

A more recent Operation Faithshare group included a Brazilian doctor whose comments have stayed in my mind. He said that our congregations were like GPs waiting for the sick to come to their surgeries.

I suspect that an analysis of the world scene would probably show that the Church is growing where there are few full time clergy, and diminishing where it is still served by a large number of clergy. That, no doubt, is a gross over-simplification and I am certainly not advocating the abolition of a 'full time ministry'.

In all fields there is a need for highly trained specialists, but not at the cost of de-skilling the majority, and certainly not so in the Church. All God's people are meant to play their part in sharing God's continuing ministry.

The Presbyterian eldership, when not merely 'ornamental and decorative', can play such a creative role, in partnership with the ministers, in breaking down the clergy/laity distinction which has so hampered the understanding of the shared ministry of all God's people. We see this in other parts of the world and we can see progress being made by many of our own sessions.

Those responsible for the deployment of ministers might take the eldership more seriously. Is the policy of creating larger units based around a 'one-person ministry' proving successful? Those who would diminish the eldership for the sake of Church unity might also think again.

Of course, the development of better inter-Church relationships is vital to the promotion of the Gospel of reconciliation. The price must not however be the heightening of the clergy-laity distinction. The eldership is an important safeguard against this.

To convince those mentioned above, elders will have to work hard at developing a more creative role.

May 1987

Questions of Money

PERHAPS ONE day I will be challenged to consider returning to the parish ministry. Let me share with you one fear I have about this. I fear the awful, exhausting problem of raising money—the money necessary to maintain the local church plant, its ministry, and its part in the wider ministry of the Church. Many congregations seem to be finding it very difficult to meet their basic commitments (let alone the development necessary for vitality) and because of this, the Kirk's Mission and Service work is in great difficulty.

On two separate occasions two leaders of different overseas churches have told me about their two offerings. The first offering is the members' expected contribution towards the agreed running costs of his/her congregation. This is not really considered as an offering. It is just a basic necessity and must be met if the person wishes to continue to be a member. The second offering is the Sunday offering —the free-will offering, the real Christian giving. I find this way of working intriguing. It releases leaders from expending time and effort on crisis appeals for money, or on coffee mornings, jumble sales, the issuing and collecting of matchboxes containing 5p pieces, the collecting of used paper, bottles and the likes. Should God's Church be reduced to such pitiful financial ploys anyway?

It could also help us to escape from what might be described as the normal static budget (*ie* last year's figure, plus a bit for inflation), a procedure which may reflect a congregation bereft of ideas.

Let's imagine that we have developed an active Christian Education Committee, Mission and Service Group, Fabric Committee, Finance Committee, Social Committee. They submit their plans for the coming year, along with their costings. The session and the congregation's representatives discuss the various proposals and draw up an agreed budget for the require-ments of the coming year—a budget which will vary from year to year according to the creativity of the different planners. Our agreed budget is then presented to the congregation, with questions and comment permitted. Let's imagine that the budget totals £35 000. If the congregation had 700 adult members the require-ment per head would be £50 in the coming year. Adjustments could be made for senior citizens, for homes where there is at present no wage earner, perhaps even for children if we were to consider them seriously as members.

For most, if not all of our adult members, £50, or some such figure, would not represent a high commitment in this day and age, but it would raise the money to meet the agreed requirements for maintenance and development and then there would be the Sunday free-will offering to develop a generous outward-looking congregation.

It seems to me that this has some merit. I have mentioned it to a few good church folk. It usually meets with a 'Yes—but' response. *Yes*—it makes sense; *but*—I don't think we could/should operate like this.

April 1983

'In oor day'

'IF IT'S a young minister he'll leave and they'll link us. If it's an old minister he'll retire and they'll link us.'

Although I appreciate that it is not an easy problem to resolve, how I wish there could be a reversal of the trend. We want to be establishing new congregations not just linking up more and more of the old ones.

In part, of course, it is a financial problem. It is expensive to try to maintain a national church with our old buildings and now traditional form of congregational life-style. Could we not, however, learn a lesson from our brethren in the United States? There there are hundreds of small congregations, as the pulpit exchange advertisements in *Life and Work* often show. These congregations are self-supporting and play their part in the wider work of their denominations because the members decide that they want their congregation to survive.

In one rural Presbytery I was told that people say—'The Kirk'll see us oot oor days' If that's true it's a sad kind of selfish discipleship and we had better come to grips with it in our sessions (and Presbyteries!). It points, not just to a financial problem, but to a spiritual poverty.

Our congregational life-style owes much to our Victorian ancestors—for the church organ, the choir, the Woman's Guild, the Boy's Brigade—things which have served the Church well. Assuming there is a future, and that we are part of it, for what will our successors look back to us, the leaders of today's Church, in gratitude?

Perhaps in some areas God is calling us to stand firm and to maintain our congregations. Perhaps in other areas he is asking us to be prepared to die in our present form to permit resurrection. In all our settings he is asking us to be creative and to meet the challenge of our age—and not just for 'oor day' only!

Recently I was working with some of the elders on the remote but lovely island of Islay where there are three ministers who have a real commitment to ministry in that kind of area. I was most encouraged to learn about the efforts going on there, and on the neighbouring island of Jura, to create a working partnership between the various sessions. Together they are planning a mission to their islands and the development of a congregational life-style which will encourage people to enquire into, and to learn and grow together in, Christian faith. The future will, I believe, look back to them with gratitude.

November 1983

Restructuring downwards

'FOR DECADES the ⸺ Church has been shrinking in terms of virtually every statistic that modern science can bring to bear upon it. Membership— down . . . Sunday school attendance—down . . . Christians at worship—down. It could be argued that Gospel statistics are of a different category but it is still factual that the Church's strategies have been based on viability, rationalisation, and restructuring downwards.'

The missing word in that quotation is 'Methodist' and it refers to the Methodist Church in New Zealand, written about in a book called *Diakonia and the Moa* by David Mullan.

In terms of the whole world-wide Church what he says is far from the reality, but you are forgiven for thinking that the quotation referred to the Church of Scotland. Many of our statistics, are not good and with many closures, unions, and linkages we are 'restructuring downwards'.

Closures run the risk of the 'two-thirds' rule—one-third of the members going to the new place of worship; one-third joining another local denomination or Christian group, one-third leaving the Church altogether.

I am not advocating a 'no closure no matter what' policy. I remember as a student conducting worship for fifteen people in an inner city congregation with a sanctuary designed to seat well over a thousand people. My then fiancée and father were asked to change their seats, having by error sat in someone's seat. That congregation died long before it was given a decent funeral!

On the other hand I know a small congregation which is struggling to stay alive through 'terminable appointments'. To lead these Christians in worship is a joy. To think of that little Christian community being closed or even united is heart-rending.

We are now seeing triple and quadruple and larger linkages. A single charge will soon be the exception! A strategy which re-structures membership into larger units so that they can support a full time paid minister is highly unlike-ly to meet the challenge we face, especially if it is based on the 'one-person ministry' idea.

What we require is new life in our congregations and an end to needless closures, needless unions, and needless linkages—and that, in human terms, lies very much in our hands as sessions, and perhaps more than many of us as elders appreciate.

April 1986

The accepted fashion

ONE DAY I met a man who told me in the course of our conversation: 'I'm a member of your congreg-ation, though I don't go very often.'

'Go' was an interesting choice of words and 'very often' had to be an overstatement. I had no memory of ever having seen the man in the church buildings.

I asked him when he was last at worship.

He had to think for a while. No, he had not been during my time with the congregation. No, he had not been during the time of my predecessor. It had been in the time of the minister before that! Together we worked it out that it had been over 10 years that this 'member' had been absent.

The length of time seemed to surprise him. He could offer no good reason. Through the years elders had called numerous times. The congregation's magazine had gone into his house month after month. All the usual invitations and appeals for support had been extended. For over 10 years he had responded with total disinterest, nor had he any intention of respond-ing otherwise—and yet he could still cheerily proclaim himself a member.

27

I remember another man. He was always at worship. He sang in the choir and often helped lead the worship. He taught in the Bible class and took part in youth weekends. I treasure many happy memories of times spent with him and his family, who were all thoroughly involved in the life and work of the congregation.

Emotional moment

Many of us would have liked to have seen this man as an elder. He clearly had the faith and the love and the leadership skills. He was an adherent. We encouraged him to make public confession of his faith. He felt that he made his profession of faith quite openly day by day and that, if he were wanted as an elder, he should be accepted as he was.

One day when some first communicants were taking their vows, he left his seat and came forward to join them. He professed his faith in the face of the congregation. I did not know he was going to do this. It was an emotional moment for both of us and for others present. Following this, his name was put on the roll of those in full communion.

He asked us to remove it. He had demonstrated his willingness to proclaim his faith in the accepted fashion, but he did not wish his name to be put on a roll in which he did not believe—a roll which it was easy to get your name on, and to retain your name on, throughout more than 10 years of absence.

November 1985

Bringing the generations together

I GET very nostalgic at Christmas when, in lots of different ways in our congregations, we celebrate the birth of Jesus. My mind returns to one of the happiest occasions in the calendar of my former congregation.

In most of our congregations, as well as the special Christmas Services, we hold Christmas parties for the children. But are 'children only' parties enough? What about the elderly, especially those who have no family around them? The festive times for the lonely can be particularly difficult. But are 'elderly only' parties enough? Should we not be thinking more about our congregations as family units and be planning events which bring the generations together?

Out of this thinking was born

our Christmas singalong. All ages came—young children, lots of teenagers, the elderly and all stages in between. It was really much more than a singalong. Our evening began in the sanctuary where we worshipped God happily together. Then all who wished to take part went through to the decorated hall for a candlelit supper—a modest but nonetheless full three-course affair, the food having been gathered collectively. It was a beautiful sight to see the family of our congregation so obviously enjoying each other's company in this setting.

After supper we entertained ourselves. It was simple homespun fun with lots of people involved in leading the entertainment. It ended with the singing of some of the songs of Christmas—hymns ancient and modern. When the benediction was pronounced, it was done so within a community which had expressed itself as a family.

From this there were developed other family occasions. The very special Easter Sunday Communion in the spring attended by our children; the summer outing after morning service to the beach, requiring two buses and a fleet of cars to transport us to the shore: the church family lunch in the autumn.

Francis Schaeffer has written: 'Our churches must be real communities . . . . They have largely been preaching points and activity generators. Community has had little place . . . . Every Christian Church should be a community which the world may look at as a pilot plant'.

There's a lot to think about in these words. You might care, in your session meeting this month, as part of your celebration of the birth of Jesus into a family, to think about how you demonstrate the family togetherness of your congregations.

December 1983

PASTORAL TOPICS

Ears that hear

ON OUR VISITS as elders we can come across very opinionated people. Perhaps we enter homes or leave them somewhat opinionated ourselves.

Come with me into the homes of two men—both, at the time, Communion attenders. The husband in the first home was very hostile to the Church and to those he viewed as its authority figures. The husband in the other home was apathetic towards the Church.

On a visit to the former, I was, at one o'clock in the morning, down a fox-hole during the last war. It took a long time to get to the source of the hostility. He shared with me his awesome

experience, an experience which happily I was too young at the time to have faced and have never had to face.

We emerged from the fox-hole. He shared his experience, in his eyes, of having been let down, served badly, by an Army chaplain. I don't know whether or not the chaplain did let the man down in some way. Perhaps he did. Perhaps he could not have done anything else in the situation. Perhaps the soldier's judgment was, not unnaturally, impaired at the time.

I do know that the man had carried the resentment of a wounded soldier throughout all the intervening years. He was not a silly man. He was, however, a man caught in an emotion which led sadly, at least in part, to his hostility towards the Church.

The other man one day walked out of a Communion service—an action considered a bit outrageous by some people. The man did not know at the time why he had so acted.

He had been brought up by a relative, the walls of whose home were covered with crucifixion scenes—scenes of blood which had frightened the man when a young boy. The brain records every experience we have ever had and every feeling we have ever felt. These recordings can be accessed.

The man had that day been sitting in a pew. He had lifted his eyes and there on the sanctuary wall in front of him there was a cross. The button was pressed on his inner tape recorder and he began to sweat, experiencing the terror feelings he had felt as a little boy. All he knew was that he had to get out of the building.

It took a lot of listening to get beneath the hostility of the one man and the apparent apathy of the other.

January 1990

Visiting the Bereaved

WHAT KIND of visits do you fear most as an elder?

I suspect, having asked many elders that question, visiting the bereaved may come quickly to your mind. What can we say to the bereaved? How can we answer their questions? Coping with their emotions can be difficult and scary. We can feel so inadequate and helpless.

31

Unintentionally, in people's lostness, silly and harmful things are said to the bereaved like 'There, there dear. It will be all right' (as if they had lost a penny down a drain!); or 'It's God's will' (I heard that once about an infant run over by a housing scheme van); or 'You shouldn't speak like that'.

Help is now being provided for elders—printed and audio-visual resources and trained resource people—and not before time. You may, however, be tempted to say: 'But it's the minister's job to comfort the bereaved.' Of course it is, but it is also the elder's job, and it is becoming clearer and clearer to me how minister and elder can, and perhaps must, work closely together in this regard.

A parish minister is likely to have quite a number of funerals to conduct—for members of the congregation and for non-members in the parish. Ministers will visit as soon as they can after hearing about the death. There will be the visits when preparations are being made for the funeral. There is the funeral itself and the follow-up visit or visits, but then it is likely that the minister will have to go through this time-consuming and demanding process with another bereaved family.

In other words, like the other members of a bereaved person's family, the minister has to leave to continue with other things. This can be when a bereaved person needs the caring attention of other people most of all. We all know that it is often after the funeral that the bereaved person can begin the agonizing process of working through the regrets, the guilts (real or imagined), the reminders that can cause so much pain, the loneliness and the difficulties involved in adapting to life without the person in whom so much had been invested.

It is in these weeks and months that the sensitive care of the district elder can be so very valuable. Remember, too, the importance of support at anniversaries (and at Christmas and New Year)—times when yesterday's memories, even the good memories, can be painful.

February 1988

Ministering to the terminally ill

LAST YEAR, when having to face up to my mortality, I don't think I was afraid of death. I trust in God about that. I did however fear greatly the possibility of having to face the situation of my family and I all knowing that we were soon to have to part. I know that for some people this can be a heart-warming enriching experience. I hope it will be so for me should I have to face it.

A family in that situation can benefit greatly from the sensitive care of a Christian elder who, amongst other things, knows that people often go through particular stages in facing up to dying.

They may begin by saying: *'No, I'm going to beat this. This isn't going to happen to me. You have got it all wrong'*. It may indeed be that the diagnosis is wrong. Most of us will know of at least one person who is still alive despite having been given a terminal sentence. Doctors must recognise their limitations, while the possibilities of co-operation with God should not be limited.

A common response can then be one of anger—*'Why me?'* A person can hit out in all directions. Ministers and elders, doctors and nurses may feel attacked, but should not take emotional attacks personally.

The next stage may be—*'Yes me, but . . .'*, and the attempt is made to bargain with God, or with life. *'Yes, I know this is happening to me but, if it can be stopped, I promise . . . (never to smoke again; to go to church every Sunday, and so on).'*

Another stage can be—*'Yes me. I know it's going to happen and I feel really bad about it'*. People may feel very depressed, not without good reason, if there is a lot they still wish to do and if there are people they feel still require their care.

If death is clearly inevitable it is good for the person to come to the stage of saying *'I'm ready'*, that is, to accept the situation and to find the peace that such acceptance can bring. We all have to learn for ourselves, and for our loved ones, that 'here we have no abiding city'.

Elders can try to help people to find their way to this acceptance and to the more that Christian faith promises. Let's beware cliches like 'It's God's will. Don't fight God', which often convey an appalling image of God and can block the emotions people may need to pass through on their way to peace.

April 1990

Modelling God's Care

SOME MONTHS ago I stressed in this column the important role the elder can play in a bereavement situation.

After the funeral, when everyone may, of necessity, have returned to their own life and concerns (including the minister who may have moved on to be with other people in the early stages of their bereavements), many a bereaved person feels very alone.

This can be the hardest time, full of negative feelings which, having been kept under control throughout the funeral, may now surface. Throughout these weeks, and perhaps months, the support of a caring elder can be a Godsend.

In my earlier column, I mentioned some 'don'ts'—like cliché talk ('There, there, dear, it will be alright'): platitudes ('It's God's will'): criticism of desperation feelings and shattered beliefs ('You shouldn't say that').

Think of any difficult situation you have ever been in, be it bereavement or something else. Did you find reponses like these helpful? Did they encourage you to go on sharing your pain with the person who made them?

The following 'do's' may be more helpful to ourselves and to the bereaved whom we visit.

We do well to recognise that there are no neat, easy, satisfactory answers to human tragedy. The mere recognition of this can help us to escape our often felt need to provide answers and solutions.

We do well to concentrate on trying to 'be with' the other person. Key to this is the basic caring skill of listening to the person. By listening I don't mean a passive, sponge-like activity. I mean an activity which really concentrates on the person, trying to get beyond what *we* think we might feel in their situation, to what the other person is actually thinking and feeling. This means the asking of questions which check out our understanding of their situation. This kind of active listening communicates genuine concern, a concern willing to try to enter into their pain. It offers acceptance and invites the other person to share more if they wish so to do.

We do well to recognise that, especially in the early stages, a question like 'Why did God allow that to happen?' is not seeking a theological answer. It is a cry of pain, in need of the support of a good listener. A hand on the shoulder may be the answer to that question. We do need to know what we believe about death so that, when the time is right, and ears can hear, and the relationship of trust established, we can share something of our faith and perhaps be able to pray with the person meaningfully.

April 1989

How often should an Elder visit his or her district?

THE ANSWER depends on what you consider to be the purpose of your visits? Clearly elders answer the question differently, as indeed do sessions.

For some the answer appears to be 'the number of times Communion cards have to be delivered'.

Such an answer tends to limit visits to the homes of 'active' members, which in a real parish setting is a considerable limitation. The lapsed can be neglected and the unchurched ignored.

It can lead to fleeting visits to the active. 'I have a lot more calls to make.' It can lead to fewer visits than the number of Communion Sundays if the person to be visited is not in and the card is 'posted' and no return visit made. It is even known for visits not to be

made to people who missed the previous Communion and who therefore still have their cards!

Of course the celebration of Communion is central to our life as Christians, but should it be the controlling factor of our pastoral work?

Personal contact

I know that the various family crises which I have gone through in the past three or four years have not occurred neatly at the Communion seasons. Visits made two or three times a year, linked to the invitation (sometimes seen as summons?) to Communion, I find hard to equate with real pastoral concern.

Should the controlling factor of our pastoral work not be our response to the various events —happy as well as unhappy—in the lives of those to whom we are called to be elders? Real personal contact is surely the aim of our pastoral work—the sharing of joys and difficulties, the giving of Christian support and love and encouragement to be actively involved in the ministry of the Church, the sharing of faith.

Sometimes at funerals I have seen elders invited to take one of the cords. At such a time I have remembered the old hymn—'Blest be the tie that binds our hearts in Christian love!'

October 1984

A caring session

QUITE OFTEN elders express to me the difficulty they are having, or have had, in getting started with their district work. A caring session will do all it can to help a new elder to understand what district visiting is about. It will also have on-going pastoral training available to its elders.

A caring session will ensure that an elder taking over a district is given every assistance possible. When you think about it, it is only

courteous, let alone caring to all concerned, to have the in-coming elder taken round the district and introduced to the people.

A new elder to a district should be made aware of sensitive information—*eg* about the death of an only child, so that a question like 'Have you any family?' can be avoided.

One of the bits of advice given in the basic eldership course is to 'take care of church workers'. Sometimes we can be a bit *careless* towards each other.

The family at the manse requires to be cared for just as much as any other family, as do the families of elders. Our families have their share of life's hurts and difficulties. It can be argued that our families need extra attention because of all the sacrifices they make to allow us to do our work as ministers and elders. As we and our families give of ourselves to other people, so we need people to give to us. A balance has to be maintained between giving and receiving.

High on our list of priorities has to be how we support each other as elders. We all have our weaknesses as well as our strengths and the need to recognise both.

The nature of our work as elders brings its sorrows and

difficulties, as well as its joys. We can all toil with feelings of inadequacy. We can all have times when the work feels too much for us. We need each other's support. This can be particularly true for the minister or elder who has no partner or family, or whose family is not supportive.

I am sure that Jesus means us to understand that one of the ways God wants to bring us support is through the love and care of our fellow elders. The minister's role in this regard is, to my mind, a pastoral priority for the minister.

A caring session will, however, devise ways to enable it as a whole to care for its elders. It will recognise that its elders differ in their pastoral ability. It might therefore consider appointing *elders' elders*—that is, carefully chosen, experienced elders who are appointed to care, not for a normal district, but for a group of elders and their families.

February 1989

'Lead me not . . .'

DO YOU ever go out into your district with the prayer, 'Lord, lead me not into deep waters'? Do you fear being asked questions about faith or having to face difficult emotional situations? Does the possibility of being asked to lead in prayer feel like a fate worse than death? Do you try to make sure that conversation is kept at a safe, chit-chat level?

Elders will respond very differently to these questions. Some of you may even resent my asking them. Many elders will, however, to some extent share these feelings.

To feel apprehensive about such matters is not unnatural. In a way it can be healthy if it prevents us from crass insensitivity and trading in platitudes. It is not healthy, of course, if it leads us into a self-imposed shallowness which does nothing for our members and can lead to feelings of frustration, even of guilt, on our part.

I believe God expects us to play our part in equipping ourselves for sharing his ministry of pastoral care. Today, perhaps more than ever before, there are resource materials and learning opportunities available to elders to help them exercise a real pastoral ministry.

37

c

But let's keep in mind that our pastoral ministry, like the ministry of every Christian, is something we do *in co-operation* with God.

It is basic to our pastoral ministry as elders that we spend time regularly with God, sharing with him our concern for the people we visit—remembering them in His presence. An important part of this is to be silent in God's presence, listening expectantly for His word to us. If we do this we may be met on more than one doorstep with: 'How did you know to come this very evening?' or 'You're just the person I wanted to see!'

We can also share our own concerns with God, openly and honestly—fears, worries, feelings of inadequacy. If we did more of this we might then not go up to a door with questions in our minds like: *What might I have to face on this call? Will I be able to cope? What if I get out of my depth?*

These questions focus on self and one's own anxieties. They can shut God out.

As we come to trust more in God's ability to be *with us* in our sharing of His ministry, we can choose to concentrate on other questions like: *What is happening in the life of this person or family? What are they feeling good or bad about?*

As we set out on our district work, questions like these can be part of our prayer and can help us to co-operate with God in His caring ministry—a ministry we are privileged to share, a ministry so needed in our society where worries and loneliness abound.

June 1989

What would you say if . . . ?

IN A RECENT 'Session Matters' column I asked you a lot of questions about how well you and your fellow elders *know* each other. Your care for each other, and your ability to work well together, hinge considerably upon your understanding of each other.

In this column I invite you to face up to some other important questions.

If, on a visit to the home of one of your members, you were asked how you can believe in the love of God in the face of the world suffering we see on television almost every evening, what would you say?

If a young person asked you to recommend a good, but not too difficult, book to help him or her

38

to understand more about the Bible, which book would you suggest?

If someone asked you what you felt Christian faith said about euthanasia, how would you respond?

What would you say to someone who asked your advice about taking a job in the nuclear arms industry?

If a non-member described himself as a Christian, not because he knew much about Christ, but because he believed himself to be a good person, what, knowing him to be a 'good' person, would you say?

If you were asked, 'What does Jesus mean to you?', what would you say in reply?

Perhaps, like me, you will find some of these questions difficult to answer in a sensitive, helpful, Christian way.

I understand that some sessions sometimes discuss issues raised in 'Session Matters'. Perhaps your session could consider these questions. You could add other questions that cause you difficulty. What to say, and when to say it, in the face of bereavement causes many of us difficulty. Perhaps you could consider the deeper question —how are we, or could we, be helping each other to be able to respond to such questions as Christian leaders?

If someone says that such questions do not arise for us as elders, then you might consider why that is so. If it is the case, there is something wrong somewhere!

October 1987

A revealing comment

THE DISTRICT ELDER is on his or her rounds. Somebody says, 'Oh, it's not *that* time already!'

Has that ever been said to you? If so, that comment gave you a number of things to ponder.

Such a comment probably meant that you were on a pre-Communion visit. It probably also pointed to the fact that the person making the comment has little sense of belonging to the congregation. He or she may dutifully accept your invitation and turn up at Communion, only to be absent again on the following Sunday.

The comment may say a lot more. It may indicate that your visits as an elder are not recognised as a genuine caring for the person you visit. Your visits may be viewed as being about getting the person to do something you want them to do, namely to attend

Communion. Your *invitation* may be viewed as a *summons*!

If our visits are carried out only on a pre-Communion basis, always linked to the delivering of Communion cards, we are unlikely to be welcomed into a home as someone recognised as having a genuine care for the people we visit.

Perhaps this is part of the reason why many of us talk about the difficulty of getting the TV turned off, let alone of sharing joys and sorrows, or talking faith and sharing a prayer.

It seems to me that our traditional linking of our visits to the pre-Communion season has *beggared* the pastoral role of the district elder. It may even have done so in our own eyes, as well as in the eyes of our members.

The elder's visit has to be about *modelling God's care*, developing a relationship which encourages our members to see in their elder a real friend—someone who cares about them, who has called in just to see them. To achieve this we have to visit at times when we have no Communion card or Free-Will Offering envelopes in our hand.

We can take a step in this direction by sharing with the minister in some of the joys and sorrows of our members—*eg* at the

40

time of baptism or on the day of a funeral.

We can develop our relationship by being there when a family has something to celebrate—a graduation, the finding of a job after redundancy and a long period of unemployment, the return of a family member from abroad. All of this implies a knowledge of what is going on in the households we visit.

A visit which begins with 'I've just popped in to say how pleased I am to hear that . . . ' may only take a few minutes, but may be worth far more than many years of only pre-Communion visits.

November 1988

Timing our visits

OFTEN ELDERS complain about the 'No Entry' sign posted on the homes of some of their members.

"Oh, no, not now......!!"

As elders we have no divine right of entry to the church homes in our district, but it is a strange church household that posts such a sign. There may be reasons for it, reasons with roots in the past; reasons which have not been properly tackled.

A session has much to think about if its elders face a lot of 'No Entry' signs. The quality and meaningfulness of its pastoral work and leadership may have to be thought about.

As a rule we should expect that a church household is open to its elder.

However, we have to consider sensitively the timing of our visits. We all know that there can be times when it is not convenient for our best friend to call! Lots of us are busy people. Crises can arise. The top current TV 'soap' can have a profound effect upon hospitality and conversation!

Most elders do their visiting in evening hours because they, and/or the people they visit, are out at work during the day. An out-of-work person, however, might very well welcome a day-time visit. Many elderly people, especially during the dark nights, do not like to open their door in the evening. Back-shift workers may not appreciate an evening visit.

If our work commitment prevents day-time visiting during the week, we may have to make use of a weekend. A session which considers its pastoral strategy in some depth may try to match up elders who are free during the day with people who prefer a day-time visit.

Early evening visits to a young family, which has bathtimes and homework to contend with, may not be appropriate. Times, however, will have to be found to meet with the children. We are their elder as well. For some people, late evening visits will not be convenient.

The timing of our visits requires care.

On the doorstep we want to ask positively —'May I come in?'; but if it is inconvenient then we must offer to return at a more convenient time.

Two simple things can help us in this regard. One is the use of the telephone to agree in advance the time of a visit. The other is the use of a visiting card which gives your name and address and telephone number, and on which can be written the time you plan to visit.

Advance notice, with the chance to make an alternative arrangement, is courteous and can be time-saving. It can also cut down on 'whistle-stop' tours!

Leaving a visiting card is also useful if you have had to call without warning and people were out. It lets them know you called. The details on it permit contact with you should the need arise.

Appointments made must, of course, be kept, or, if absolutely necessary, contact must be made to explain your enforced change of plan.

January 1989

'I just told my Elder ...'

YOU ARE IN a member's home. Eventually the conversation gets round, if not to the sharing of faith, at least to church matters.

Someone starts to get critical. On Sundays the prayers are too long. The sermon is boring. Perhaps the minister or a fellow-elder comes in for criticism about some mistake he or she is said to have made in a particular situation. Faced with this, what do you say or do?

Test this out for yourself. When you are being negatively and hurtfully critical about someone or something, you may sound thoroughly rational and objective, but inside, beneath it all, you are feeling bad about something. When you are at peace, when you are feeling happy, you sometimes cause hurts by mistake, but you do not do so intentionally.

If this is true, then, when faced with hostile criticism, we need to try to get beneath the surface to the feelings. It may be that the critic had a bad experience long ago during the war, and felt God had not met their need. This bad feeling has been nursed and fed throughout all the intervening years and on this pastoral visit it has surfaced for those with eyes to see and ears to hear.

It may be that the person had a particularly good relationship with a previous minister or elder and is going through the process of bereavement and has not yet been able to adapt to the new situation.

Perhaps the person sees himself as a 'failure' at his work situation and has longed, without success, to achieve some status in the life of the congregation.

We need to help the person to get in touch with the real feelings which underlie the bitter criticism —and to confront him or her, gently, in time, with the real issues.

Constructive criticism, which will be conveyed in an entirely different spirit, we will welcome. As my friend, the late Norman Swan, once wrote: 'We who sit in the pews are not to be regarded as amiable peasants, uninterested in Christian plans and with little to offer'. We can receive constructive criticism—without disloyalty to our fellow church leaders or to the critic himself.

It would be hard, however, to over-emphasise the importance of loyalty to one's fellow-elders, past as well as present. This is not to say that we have to defend each other as pure and faultless human beings, which clearly we are not.

But it is to say that we take care not to fuel the winter of people's discontent. Even our interested silence can be used as fuel. 'I just told my elder what I thought. He didn't disagee with me.'

December 1984

'See what you made me do!'

I AM a fan of the Peanuts cartoons.

In one of them Charlie Brown's friend Lucy says that she never thinks about the past, nor does she worry about the future. Lucky her, if we are to believe her. Charlie Brown asks her about her present.

Lucy replies: 'The present drives me crazy!'

How are you feeling about your present as an elder, as we start a new year?

I hope it is not driving you crazy, but you may be feeling a bit jaded. You may not be getting the fulfilment in the eldership that you had hoped for. The relationship with some of the members of your district may not be what you would dearly like it to be.

As we see in other cartoons, Lucy demands of life only 'ups'. She resents 'downs'. When the 'downs' come she blames life. It is the present's fault that she feels what she feels—and she blames, complains, resents, which is a typical child reaction. How often have we heard a child say—'See what you made me do!' or "You made me feel bad'? A child has to learn that we do our own feeling.

Matter of choice

The external circumstances of our present may *invite* us to feel this or that, but we choose what we feel and what we do with the feelings we *choose*.

Perhaps someone says to me: 'I didn't like your recent Session Matters column. It was a poor piece of work. I got nothing from it.' I will have a choice to make. I may choose to feel crushed and decide never again to write the column. Or, I may choose to accept the criticism and to try a lot harder next time. I may on the other hand choose to question my critic's judgment. The fact that the person didn't like the column, and didn't get anything from it, may have more to do with the critic than with what was written.

The comment made to me has invited me to feel something, possibly to feel bad, but the choice is mine as to what I will do with it.

Next time you come away from a pastoral visit, or possibly even a session meeting, with some negative feelings, consider carefully the invitation with which you were presented and the choice you have made regarding your feeling. You may find a better choice then faces you.

January 1986

'The real thing'

FOR MANY of our members, only the minister's visit is a 'real' visit. Even the visit of an assistant minister, or one made by a deaconess, may not be thought of as being on the same plane as that made by the minister. Is this because we who are ministers have, or are thought to have, a monopoly of Christian understanding and of spirituality and caring skills?

Do you as an elder consider your pastoral visits to be 'real' visits or do you consider them pale imitations of the real thing? To think that would be, for me, a sad view for anyone to take about the elder's visit, assuming that we are not talking about whistle-stop Communion card distribution.

Quite often in the pages of *Life and Work* we read the plea for a return to the good old days when ministers were said to visit more often. For many reasons times change. Job descriptions may have to alter to face new situations. People's different talents may call for the making of different priorities.

Real visits

Different geographical factors certainly make different demands. A large congregation and/or a large parish, where the non-Church feel free to call on the services of the parish minister, can lead to ministers conducting two or three funerals in a week (with all the follow-up visits), let alone time spent with wedding couples, families wanting baptism, and people going through crises.

What does not vary, however, is the need for a genuine expression of continuing concern for our members on the part of those who are called and appointed, indeed ordained, to lead the ministry of the congregation. Elders are ordained to be part of this and their visits must be 'real' visits.

We must make them so to encourage in our congregations the New Testament understanding of shared ministry. We might help break the talent burying understanding of the ministry as being the work of the person we call 'the minister'.

When we consider a fair-sized congregation, not only its active roll but also its supplementary roll, *and* all in the parish who are not members of the Church, there is much 'real' visiting for us to do. There is also much need for us to call on the services of our fellow-members to help in this shared ministry. A congregation motivated to do this will be doing the real thing.

May 1986

Getting the message

I KNEW on Saturday it would be Frank's birthday. Frank was an elder. He used to call me his 'boy minister', with I think no disrespect intended. After all, half a century separated us in age at the time.

On the Saturday afternoon, I visited Frank. For quite a time we sat at his fireside and talked about this and that. It was pleasant. I remember that someone else called in to wish him a happy birthday. After the person had gone, we talked on for a bit and then I began to take my leave.

As I was getting up, I sensed that Frank had something to say. I can't remember what he said. Perhaps he didn't say anything, but somehow I knew he had something else to say. As I slowly eased myself back down in the chair, the old man started to speak and I knew that the visit, the real meeting, was about to begin. On his 80th birthday I got the story of his life—his joys and sorrows, the pleasures and disappointments he had experienced. It was heart-warming.

Our visits as elders shouldn't be controlled by Communion card delivery. Just as we look to our fellow-members for support on important church occasions, so we should pay attention to them at

45

D

their times of importance—and not just the times of difficulty, also the times of celebration and the land- marks like my friend Frank's 80th birthday.

People need attention. It is often said that one of the most caring things we can do for another person is really to listen to them.

Jesus said, tellingly, 'He who has ears to hear, let him hear.' We have to learn to hear what is said, not what we think is going to be said, but what is actually being said. It can be helpful to feed back to the person what he or she has said so that we know we have heard accurately and the person knows himself/herself truly heard. And we need to hear what is *not* being said, or being half-said, or being said to camouflage the real message. Listening is an art!

Jesus also said, 'He who has eyes to see, let him see.' Listening with our eyes is important. The way people (including ourselves!) sit, stand, massage imaginary pains, avert our eyes, furrow our brow, and much else—'body lang- uage' as it is now called—all speak to us and help us, if we have the eyes to see, to understand each other.

I am grateful that that Saturday afternoon I got the message, the plea, and the invitation to listen.

May 1985

46

The flexibility principle

HAPPILY THE understanding of the session as the leadership team of the congregation is becoming more widely recognised, held and worked at. Important to it is the principle of flexibility. People have to be able to cover for each other and to move into new positions when the situation calls for it.

Does your session apply this flexibility principle in its pastoral work? Or does it apply the rigidity principle of giving the newest elder the most recently vacated district and leaving him/her to get on with it?

Consider, we are not all equally competent at caring meaningfully for the elderly, the young, married couples and families, teenagers, the lapsed, the non-members . . . .

Nor does the chemistry work for us in all households. I get on well with some people. With others I find it more difficult. Some people get on well with me, others don't, while others can take me or leave me! I suspect this is true of most, if not all, ministers—and elders—and certainly so if our relationships with our members go beyond superficial chit-chat.

The flexibility principle can help.

'Victim!'

Imagine an elder who cannot make any headway with the Jones family. No matter what he/she tries, there is no positive response and the Jones family and the church grow further and further apart. If nothing more creative is done, Mr and Mrs Jones are likely to become two more additions to the Supplementary Roll.

With a more flexible pastoral strategy it could be possible for a fellow elder to visit the Jones in exchange perhaps for a call which that elder finds fruitless.

The strategy of an area team of elders can help with this. Calls can be exchanged, difficulties shared and some progress can be made regarding the matching of skills to the different categories mentioned above.

I would very much welcome hearing about any efforts being made by creative sessions to put into effect the flexibility principle.

March 1987

YOU ARE visiting a lady who has a particular problem. As her elder she asks you for help. You make a suggestion. 'Yes', she says 'that could be an answer. I'll think about that. But you see . . . .'

She has appreciated your suggestion, but it isn't quite right. You try again. After all you're an elder. People are supposed to be able to turn to you for help.

The lady smiles and nods her head. You sigh a sigh of relief. Your second suggestion is an improvement. 'Yes', she says, 'but you see . . . .'

Your second solution, like the first, has been inadequate. You begin to feel uneasy. You ride to the rescue with a third suggestion. 'Perhaps you could . . . .'

'Yes', she says, 'but . . . .'

Do you recognise this situation?

What are you to do? Try again to provide a solution? It isn't going to work, is it? Consciously or unconsciously you are being played with. The lady is playing the role of a *victim*. She is inviting you to play the role of a rescuer, but no matter what you say or suggest, she is going to say 'Yes, but . . . .'

If she is more emotionally disturbed and you keep riding to

47

the rescue with 'solution' after 'solution', she may eventually say—'See, nobody can help me. Not even the Church!' Now you feel really put down. Perhaps she says—'I thought you (her elder) would be able to help me'. Now the *victim* has become a *persecutor* and the *rescuer* has become the *victim*.

The visit comes to an end. You both part full of bad feelings.

You will be aware that there is a whole new initiative going on in the Church today to provide elders with training opportunities, including help and understanding in dealing more effectively with situations like these.

In Alcoholics Anonymous circles, it has long been known that an alcoholic cannot be *'rescued'*. His or her co-operation is essential. *'Rescuing'* and *'helping'* are not the same thing.

Have a look at John 5:1-8, where Jesus asks that strange question to the man at the pool —'Do you want to get well?' Not everybody does.

People with real and deep problems cannot be 'rescued', but they can be loved and helped to pick themselves up if they want to.

Faced with the kind of illustration of the lady, if it seemed appropriate, you might pray with

her, and together in prayer offer the problem to God, seeking his *help*, his support of the lady as she wrestles with her problem, and of you with whom the problem has been shared.

August 1985

Conflicting loyalties

IN *COX: Practice and Procedure in The Church of Scotland,* we read:

'As "pastors and doctors" should be diligent in sowing the seed of the Word, so the elders should be careful in seeking the fruit of it in the people,' and that, *'the office of elders is severally and conjunctly to watch over the flock committed to their charge, both publicly and privately, that no corruption of religion or manners enter therein.'*

Apart from the old-fashioned language, that sounds good, although we may feel a bit uneasy about the 'corruption' bit. Our unease may be increased when told that 'elders ought to bring to the session things they cannot correct by private admonition'.

We tend to shy away from this in a way that previous generations did not. In a more puritanical age we dealt as elders with 'scandals' like swearing, cursing, profaning the Lord's Day, drunkenness, and sexual sins. 'Discipline' was high on our agenda. Should it be so today? Perhaps it should, but in no way would I wish to return to the days when, for example, unmarried mothers took their infants for baptism to what was considered the more kindly Episcopal Church—'the Kirk where they baptize a' the bairns', or to the days when ministers were reprimanded for 'promiscuous invitations' to Communion.

Few of us would wish to return to the days which gave the Kirk such a stern and negative image, but what are we to do with members who belong to our congregation but who demonstrate remarkably little interest in its life and witness, including its Sunday worship? If we have done our best to surface the real issues, and have offered whatever help we can to no avail, what then?

Cox tells us that *'the Kirk Session shall have power, at the annual revision of the Communion roll, to remove from the roll the names of persons who are giving no evidence of read interest or are taking no share in the Church's work and worship'*.

Many sessions and elders feel very hesitant about this exercise of 'discipline' and so our Communion rolls often contain the names of many who are showing 'no real interest . . . .'

It seems to me that we have a problem of conflicting loyalties. There are members who are over-burdened or disheartened because of the lack of support from the 'no clear interests', and members who might become more involved but for the 'witness' of the disinterested. Our acceptance of the standards of the 'no clear interests' does not help them themselves to take the Faith and Church membership seriously.

Perhaps the most serious of all is the obstacle the 'no clear interests' may present to the encouragement of those outside the Church. It is not easy to persuade someone to become interested in Christ and his Church when he watches a neighbour, who is a 'member', cutting the lawn on Sunday mornings except on the odd Communion Sunday.

October 1985

"SAY ONE FOR ME..!"

Members who aren't very interested

DO YOU have quite a number of members in your district who want to continue to belong to your congregation, but who demonstrate remarkably little interest in its life and witness, including its Sunday worship?

If so, what can we do about it? Sessions up and down the land are wrestling with this problem. Where they are not doing so, the situation is bleak.

A temptation, of course, is to come on like a 'heavy parent', emphasising the 'oughts' and 'shoulds', stressing the vows our members once took and have not rescinded. And it's true. They did take vows, and vows should be kept. A promise is a promise. The heavy parent approach may work (if that's the right word) with a few, but most adults had enough of that approach a long time ago and are not likely to respond well to it now.

Jesus had some very forthright and blunt things to say to religious leaders about the value of some of the 'oughts' they sought to impose, but his was not the way of the heavy parent.

We are more likely to succeed by means of a genuinely caring approach—one which does not seek to avoid the issues, but rather, getting alongside the person, seeks to go beyond the excuses and the criticisms to the real reasons for the non-participation.

For many of our members, their vows were taken a long time ago. Their contract with God and the Church may have been ill-prepared for in poorly-led first communicant classes. The sessions that admitted them may have expressed the contract in light-weight terms. It can be the case that, following a good communicants class where faith, enthusiasm, and commitment have been fostered and demonstrated, the poverty of the life-style of the congregation has drained away the enthusiasm and commitment.

Some of our members may have been dealt some heavy blows in life. They may not wish to leave the Church but do not see its relevance in the face of these blows.

Some of our 'members' may in fact be no different from, though less honest than those who do not belong because they do not have the faith to belong. If this is the case, then let's encourage this to come out into the open.

Perhaps the telling phrase

above is 'which does not seek to avoid the issues'. How often on our visits have we avoided the issues? If we are not to go on doing so, we may need to spend more time together as elders coming to grips with various issues and learning how to engage with people relevantly and caringly on the issues.

September 1985

The District Elder

IN THE pamphlet *The Office of the Elder in the Church* (The Saint Andrew Press), which was written before women were ordained to the eldership, we read: *To each elder there is normally assigned a district. . . .*

Unfortunately 'normally' should read 'almost invariably'!

. . . for the oversight of which he (and now she) is responsible. . . .

That old word 'oversight' is to be understood within the context of the shared ministry of the whole congregation.

He should assist the minister in the care of . . . .

'Assist' can be viewed as a dignifying word. Elders share fully in pastoral care, along with the minister. It is not to be translated into the subservient role of merely assisting the (real) minister. District elders have a ministry in their own right to care for their district. This care is not just about caring for our people, but about enabling our members to care, to be the minsters they are called to be.

. . . the sick, the aged and the needy . . .

The term 'needy' is a wide term. There are the financially needy, the emotionally needy (*eg* the lonely, of which there are so many), the spiritually needy. YTS young people, the unemployed. The redundant are needy people. People whose beliefs and values lead to violent or self-destructive behaviour are needy people. 'Needy' is a wide term!

. . . and in encouraging those outside the fellowship of the Church

We have a missionary task in our parish, beyond the homes of our members. This missionary task exists very much in the homes of our members where husband or wife may not belong to the fellow-ship of the Church. In many of our Church homes there are young people who may have been baptised, but who do not belong to the fellowship in a conscious and living way. The challenge to us is to try to help people to take seriously Jesus and what he tells us about life.

To be a sensitive and caring district elder is quite a calling.

February 1990

An evening a week?

IF WE think in terms of real pastoral concern, lots of issues arise for us.

With how many homes can I be expected to develop a meaningful pastoral relationship? What I can tackle may be different from what you can tackle. What I can tackle may differ at different times in my life.

Do I require some help, training if you like, to help me to see and hear what is unsaid, to help me be more sensitive to different kinds of problems, to help me get *beyond the weather* in my conversation, even possibly help me to get beyond the doorstep itself!

It may be that some of us are more suited to working with young couples, while others are more effective with the elderly or with the lapsed. Is there a need for specialisation?

Sessions could think more creatively about their pastoral strategy.

However it is done, if a district is given to you, real pastoral concern requires time. How much time? Should the work output of an elder not be at least as much as that of a BB officer or Sunday school teacher—that is at least an evening a week?

In any given month this may mean an evening spent at the session meeting and possibly another at the meeting of the congregational board, which leaves two or three evenings in the month for our pastoral work.

Perhaps one of these evenings could be given to a district gathering or house group which brings our district together in fellowship.

I can hear you say: 'But what about all the other things I do for the Church? I give far more than one evening a week!'

Many elders do. Perhaps more of them should be elders without districts or with very small districts. Perhaps we need a more active policy of participation in the congregation so that the elders are not made to carry too many responsibilities. We may have priority decisions to make. Perhaps things of less consequence have to be dropped to permit the development of real pastoral concern on the part of the session.

November 1984

In at the deep end

Should an elder pray when he visits a house in his district?

IF BENEATH this question there lies the question of whether an elder should ever pray in the homes of his/her district, I would believe the answer is a clear affirmative. Christians should be able to pray together. It would be hard to disagree with that. So why should those who have been ordained as the spiritual leaders of a congregation not be permitted to pray with their fellow-members in their districts? Indeed they should be willing and able to do so.

I don't think we should, however, make a law out of a means of Grace. There may be times when it is not appropriate to lead a prayer on a visit. Faced by a non-member husband, who resents his wife's involvement in the congregation,

might not be the time. On the other hand, it might be just the time. My experience tells me that there are far more people who welcome being led in prayer than I, at one time, would have believed. We must remember, however, that this is not something we, to satisfy our needs and self-expectations, do to others regardless of their needs and wishes.

If we haven't done this before, what's the best way to start?

Perhaps in your district you have a housebound member who is no longer able to take his/her place in the pews, no longer able to hear the Scriptures read at a service of Worship. Remind that person that he is still very much part of God's family. Ask if he would like you to read a passage of Scripture with him—perhaps the 23rd Psalm. Few will decline the invitation. After the reading —quietly, simply and sincerely —lead a prayer thanking God for the faith offered to us in that psalm; for our belonging to the Church, and for his blessing on your fellow-member and yourself.

You may find that, following this, your visit begins. If, however, you leave at that point, you will have made a pastoral visit, having pointed your fellow-Christian to his or her God.

Perhaps a new family has come into your district. Before you leave on your first visit you could suggest that together you ask for God's blessing on their new home. You might read Jesus' teaching, at the end of the Sermon on the Mount, about building a house on rock rather than on sand. Ask for God's blessing on this new home, giving thanks for the privilege you have of being part of it, and seeking God's help to ensure that its foundations are firmly based.

I don't know what the 'best way to begin' is. I do know that if we are to learn to swim, we must get into the water—and we must get more than our toes wet!

January 1985

Letters and cards

'SESSION MATTERS' is very much a personal column. Through it I share things dear to my heart about the eldership, about our collective work as a session and often about some aspect of the district work entrusted to most elders.

This month's column is a particularly personal one. Throughout the past year I have been involved in minor (so-called) and major surgery. There is a difference! I have also been engaged in a battle against lymphoma, which is a kind of cancer. The battle is very much with the chemotherapy treatment and its effect.

During the course of this, I received a card with the following written on it: *May your operation go well and you will soon be on the road to recovery. Best wishes and assurance of prayer.*

The card was signed 'A Session Matters fan'. Whoever you are, dear reader, I am grateful to you. Your card meant a lot to me as have the cards and letters received from sessions and Presbyteries for whom I have worked.

As you may appreciate, it is no easy thing to be so ill, especially for someone like me who has had a 40-year-long phobia about hospitals.

The experience has taught me many things, including some very simple things—so simple that they can be so easily missed—like, for example, the power of a card or a letter to someone going through a difficult time. Having never experienced such a difficult time, I have not fully appreciated the value of a card or letter which lets a person know that people care and wish him or her *well*: that they and others are praying for you. It is moving and so helpful when people convey what you have meant and still mean to them, *ie* when the cards and letters are truly personalised.

I can think back to people who have been in some difficulty, and though I was concerned for them and included them in my prayers, I didn't communicate my concern to *them*. Often this will have been because I did not appreciate the nature of their difficulty.

I invite you to think about the people in your district, non-Church members as well as Church members, and the value which a card or letter from you could be to them when they are in some difficulty. You might also encourage other people in the congregation to share in this ministry through card and letter.

Think, too, about a long illness, which is akin to a bereavement, a loss situation. It is not just at the start of the difficulty that your ministry is needed.

Nor, remember, is the difficulty necessarily the person's alone. It is usually shared by family and close friends who might also be helped by this form of ministry.

September 1989

Caring for those in hospital

IT DEPENDS a lot on how you view the role of 'the minister' as to how much you think his or her time should be devoted to visiting people who are not ill, or bereaved, or in any difficulty.

No doubt we would agree that the minister should be around when people are in real difficulty. I hope we would also agree that, at such times, there is also a genuine ministry for the elder to exercise, in his or her own right, especially regarding someone in the elder's own district.

In the previous column I spoke about the value of the ministry an elder can carry out through cards and letters. In this column I invite you to think about someone in your district going into hospital.

55

If the patient is not too ill, and conversation is proving difficult for patient and family, because of their lack of news while their life revolves around visiting hours, the elder can help to oil the wheels of conversation for patient and family alike. In such a situation it could be useful for us to encourage other people also to visit.

Care has to be taken in hospitals which permit long visiting periods. Patients can be more exhausted by their visitors than by their illness! Visiting in times of serious illness certainly requires far more from us than mere time-filling chatter until we can find a way of taking our leave.

If visiting times are limited to an hour in the afternoon and an hour in the evening, and if the patient is seriously ill, it may not be appropriate for us to use up any of the time needed by the patient and his or her nearest and dearest. But it would be nice to think the elder belonged to the 'nearest and dearest'.

A golden rule is to contact the family, to express one's concern, and to ask for permission to visit at an appropriate time, and to take no offence if our offer is declined until the time is considered to be appropriate. Letters and cards can more than suffice until that time comes.

A letter or card can also be an appropriate way of making our offer. In times of serious illness the family can be exhausted by the phone ringing all evening after they return from visiting hour. We shall also want to find ways of expressing our concern for the patient's nearest and dearest who are also going through a difficult and anxious time.

Caring can require more thought and ingenuity than often we demonstrate.

October 1989

Prayer for and with

I KNOW that it says in *Cox: Practice and Procedure in the Church of Scotland* that it is no part of the regular duties of an elder to pray with the sick in his or her district. Presumably to read Scripture in such a context would also be wrong.

There are aspects of the eldership of yesterday best left in the past, but it is sad how in this century we have reduced the eldership. However, since the mid-fifties, bit by bit the status and role of eldership has been being reclaimed, albeit slowly, in Scotland. In this regard the elders in the so-called 'Third World' put us to shame.

When someone quotes the above pieces of *Practice and Procedure* to me, I ask: Is it all right for two Christians to read a piece of Scripture together? Is it all right for two Christians to pray with each other? If the answer to these questions is in the affirmative, that such activities are not limited to a select few, then how can it be wrong for an elder to do such things with members of the congregation?

Is an elder not a *spiritual* leader of a congregation and rightly ordained to the ministry of *leadership*? If so, how can prayer with other people be no part of his or her pastoral care?

Prayer, like marriage and other relationships, like sex, like money and many other good and valuable things in life, can be misused and abused. As with so many of God's gifts, there are things to be learned about how to use the gifts so that they become the gifts God means them to be. And so it is with prayer—with our whole conversation with God, including our prayers *for* other people, and our praying *with* people.

At the beginning of this year I was in hospital for major surgery. There were times when I was so low that I only wanted my family with me during the two separate hours of visiting permitted each day. Many ministers visited me, but happily they could visit outwith these two hours. Would the day come when an elder received similar recognition and privilege!

I appreciated many a reading and prayer led by my ministerial colleagues.

One Saturday afternoon I was visited by my session clerk of over 10 years ago. I feel the emotion in my throat even as I write this. It was not emotionally easy to see my friend Tom as I faced up to the fact of my mortality. Nor, I know well, was it easy for him, for we love one another.

Before he left, he asked if he could read a passage of Scripture with me. I agreed and he stood by the side of my bed and read from the Old Testament, about God's promise to his servant to be with him throughout the building of the Temple of Jerusalem. The reading was, like the visit itself, Tom's prayer *for* and *with* me. I shall never forget the ministry of that elder to this minister.

November 1989

57

ELDERSHIP

'Knowing each other'

I INVITE you to think about the members of the session you belong to. Assuming that you are sitting comfortably and safely as you are reading your *Life and Work*, take a moment or two to think about your fellow elders. Close your eyes and visualise each of them.

Did you miss any of them out? Are you uncertain about some of their names?

If you belong to a small session, and especially if you have been on session for some considerable time, your answer to these questions may well be 'of course not!' If you belong to a large session your answer may be 'Yes' to both the questions.

But consider, even if you know all of their names, how well do you know them as people? Do you know their life situations, their joys and enthusiasms, their difficulties and sorrows, why they tend to behave in this or that way? Without this kind of knowing our work of leading the congregation together will be impaired.

Do you know what your fellow elders feel about their eldership? Are they enjoying it? Do any of them feel over-burdened? Are some being imposed upon by being allowed to carry more than their fair share of the work? Are any taking on more church work than they should for their own good, their family's good, the Church's good?

Understanding

Do some of them feel out of their depth in their district work— feeling inadequate in bereavement situations, in situations where they know there is a need to put their faith into words, or whatever?

Without this kind of knowing of one another, how can we care for each other, *be* the Church to each other?

On a district visit something happened to one elder. It so shattered him that he resigned. Whether or not the resignation could have been prevented at the time, I do not know. What I do know is that it was many years later that some of his former fellow-elders found out what had led to the resignation. Had their session been more aware of each other, the experience might have been shared at the time and the pain level for the person concerned reduced.

Do you feel known, understood and valued by your fellow-elders? Do they feel known, understood, loved by you and by each other?

September 1987

Are we 'Scots or Christians'?

ONCE ON a training programme with the session, of which I had the privilege to be the moderator, we were divided up into pairs and invited to share our loneliest moment.

My fellow-elder shared with me a visit he had made to someone dear to him who was terminally ill. He was visibly moved. I had actually shared this experience. I had shared the visit with my friend. But at the time I had never realised what it was costing him.

There was a lot of emotion in the room as we shared such times together in our pairs. We did this under the skilled leadership of Dr Archie Mills and after we had gone through many other training programmes at a less intensive level. I am not advocating that such sharing is suddenly sprung upon a session, but that it is worked towards.

On training programmes I often offer elders the opportunity to share a 'good' and a 'bad' visit, or likes and dislikes about being an elder. The experience has always, to date, been felt to be worthwhile. The sharing produces feelings of

59

encouragement, togetherness, support, warmth. It is strange therefore that, when I ask them about such an experience in the life of their session, the answer is often in the negative. At this point I recall Archie's plea: 'What do you want to be, Scots or Christians?'!

So often all that we share (those of us who have the courage to speak out in the sometimes large group session meeting) is our opinions. We may respect people for the quality of their thinking, but we grow to love people with whom we can share feelings, and so come to know and be known at a deeper level than is afforded by chit-chat and opinions.

I remember an elder saying at a training programme—'I have shared more with a fellow-elder in the last five minutes of sharing than I have in the past five years'.

I remember that time of sharing with Bobby as though it were but yesterday, and the warmth remains.

A session in which the members are helped to know and love each other will transact its business better. And it will be better equipped to encourage and enable its congregation to go and do likewise.

May 1987

'Once an elder . . .'

SOME SAY: 'Once an elder, always an elder'.

Others say that an elder's term of office should be limited as the appointment of a manager to the congregational board is limited: that there should be a fixed term of office.

In the Church of Scotland an elder is *ordained*, which signifies that we consider the appointment to the eldership to be on a different plane from, say, the appointment of a manager to the congregational board.

To accept ordination is to take a most serious step and to enter upon a most important office within the Church of Scotland. A person is ordained into a particular session to exercise, along with fellow-elders, a spiritual leadership within a particular congregation. Such a step is not to be taken lightly or from selfish motives, but with reverence and dedication. The vows taken are, in my view, akin to the vows of marriage and are just as long-term in their intention. We do not enter marriage on a three-year term of appointment basis, renewable or otherwise!

An elder can, of course, be removed from office. He or she

can resign from his session and retain status as an elder as long as the resignation is simply accepted. An elder can also demit his status as an elder by making his request to his session and by having the petition granted. This is possible, but it is surely not the intention for one who accepts the vows of ordination to the eldership.

Mamie was a senior citizen by the time she was ordained to the eldership. She was fit and active and a gem of a Christian woman. She belonged to a team eldership. The session as a body was a team, but it also operated in area teams. Each elder had a district but worked with two or three other elders in a shared concern for their combined districts. Mamie belonged to her area team.

As time went by she was less and less able to visit her district. Evening calls, calls up flights of stairs, became impossible. Others in the team took over these calls. Eventually Mamie had no pastoral calls to make, but she never left the team. The team would arrange for their monthly house group to be held in Mamie's house, or they would transport Mamie, and indeed others who wanted to take part, to wherever the group was meeting in the area. Likewise she was brought to session meetings where she contributed to our life by her presence and her warm support.

A few years ago Mamie died. Her funeral service was conducted in the sanctuary of her church. Her coffin was surrounded by all her fellow-elders—her brothers and sisters, her sons and daughters in the faith. Truly it was a rich family occasion. She had never resigned. She had not even retired. She died an active elder. We would not have wanted it otherwise for her—or for ourselves.

August 1983

'Burn-out'

AS YOU will know, there is a lot of concern in the Church at the moment about what is termed 'ministerial burn-out'. It prompts one to ask—How does your session care pastorally for the person or family who lives in the manse?

I remember my early days as a parish minister when, with Shakespeare's Shylock I felt 'prick me I bleed'—a feeling you may sometimes also share as a district elder.

I wonder what the 'elder burn-out' rate is.

We feel the object of the prayer 'Bless Thy minister and elders, our servants'.

What a difference it makes when as members of session we get to know each other at the level of our feelings and shared experience, the soil in which love for one another can flourish.

Depth of caring

One of my most treasured memories is of conducting a particularly difficult funeral. I was trying to be God's servant to a family who had lost their son in a tragic accident. By the time this happened, love and understanding had become something very real for us as elders. By then my fellow-elders knew what it cost me to try to minister in this kind of situation.

I will never forget the family standing in the front row, holding each other up and singing 'On Christ the solid rock I stand, all other ground is sinking sand'—the hymn we had chosen together. Nor will I ever forget the presence, not just of the family's elder, but of 50 per cent or more of the session, present to be a strength to me, to minister to me.

After the service, Andrew returned to his factory. Fifteen minutes after his shift ended, around 10.15 pm if I remember correctly, there was a knock at the manse door. The manse elder had called just to check up on how I was feeling—the incarnation of the prayer 'Bless our minister. Thy servant'.

With more of this kind of depth of caring for one another, there would be far less need to talk of 'burn-out' regarding ministers or elders—or indeed of members of our congregations.

March 1986

Counting the cost

IN AN EARLIER column about our pastoral work as elders I suggested that the work of an elder should be at least as much as that of a BB officer or Sunday school teacher, that is, over and above our Sunday duties, at least an evening a week devoted to our work as leaders of a congregation board. In an average month this could mean participation in the session meeting and that of the congregational board. A valuable evening could be spent in a district (or combined districts) house group. One or perhaps two evenings could be given over to district work, thus unshackling pastoral care from pre-Communion visits only.

Do I hear you say that you already give far more than an evening a week as it is? It may be that you are also a BB officer, Christian Action group leader or whatever and whatever. Perhaps your husband or wife often says: 'Why don't you just take your bed down to the church halls?'

Is it right that you are doing so much? Is it a good management (stewardship) of your time?

Perhaps elders who are given heavy, time-consuming responsibilities in the congregation, or who are playing a major role as Christians in life beyond the congregation, should be offered a small district or no district at all, for their own good and the good of a district they may not be able to care for pastorally. Perhaps as

sessions, and as individuals, we have decisions about priorities to face up to.

Come with me to the AGM of a congregation's men's club—a fun club, carpet bowls and the likes. A man is being pushed into becoming its treasurer. He doesn't want the job, but no one else is willing, despite the fact that few of them give much time to the working life of the congregation.

Unfair burden

The man is a good elder. He has his session and board meetings to attend. He has his district to care for. He is a Bible class leader and does much else to help his congregation. He has his every-

day work and, not least of all, his family to look after and be with. Here he is being almost bullied into taking on yet another commitment. The whole thing is very unfair. If the club cannot produce a treasurer for its lightweight activity without placing another burden on a fine elder, I question its value in the life of the congregation.

We may have to make value judgments and say no to some involvements—even if it means that this or that in the life of the congregation has to collapse—so that time and energy can be given to what matters more.

A mistake we can, consciously or unconsciously, make is that of holding all the jobs in the hands of a few. An analysis of this can be quite sobering. Try it out for yourself. Sometimes the few want it so. They need it so. You can watch various congregations slowly dying in the hands of such leaders who do not even begin to grasp that Christian leadership is about encouraging and enabling the ministry of others.

Of course it isn't always easy to obtain the help of others, especially after years of the control of the few, and so we opt for the line of least resistance. Someone resigns from a not too onerous task. An

elder has just retired. He is asked to take on the task. He already has at least one other demanding job in the life of the congregation on top of his eldership, but it is easier to ask him than to go out into the congregation and find someone not already overly committed. If the elder agrees, as so often we do, the few have again added to their burden, at cost to family, to health, to the more important aspects of our calling as elders, and at the cost of many in our congregations who do not feel needed and wanted at the heart of the working life of the congregation.

April 1985

Sabbatical leave

SOME TIME ago the Church of Scotland's creative Committee of Forty recommended that elders should be offered sabbatical periods, that is periods of release from their normal duties and responsibilities in the life of the congregation. The Church is beginning to recognise the importance of this for its pastors, so why not also for its elders?

It seems to me that this would be a better move than the sometimes-made suggestion that elders should only serve, like members of the congregational board, for a fixed term of office. I know that our sister-denominations in America have elders on fixed terms of office but I don't personally believe in it.

What seems to me to be important about a sabbatical period is that it is not just release from duties for say six months or a year. That would be a somewhat negative approach to it.

Rather, it is a time that should be programmed and used to re-charge the elder's batteries—a time for the elder to so some learning and experiencing, to help him or her to return to full duties with new ideas and renewed enthusiasm.

With the moderator, and perhaps the help of one or two elders made responsible for sabbatical periods, the elder could be helped to work out a study programme—to include reading material (eg Bible study, books about our faith and its impli-cations, material on eldership), and participation in a 'Training in Elder-ship' course held by the Presbytery (in 1985 some 31 Presbyteries held some kind of a course) and in one of the residential courses held at Carberry Tower or St Ninian's, Crieff.

Possibly the elder could engage in a study of some particular pers-onal interest or undertake a piece of research about the Church, local,

national or international.

It would be important for the elder to have some means of sharing what he/she is doing and, I think, crucial that he/she continues to attend session meetings to keep fully in touch with what is going on.

Such a programme would take organisation on the part of the session—working out the rota, ensuring the elder's respon-sibilities were being covered, and assisting with the particular elder's sabbatical programme and its costs.

A creative session would be able to achieve this. I would hope it could receive help from its local Presbytery education committee, and centrally it could look to the help of the Kirk's Eldership Working Party.

February 1986

The absent friends

AN ACTIVE, caring and creative session will meet regularly, most likely monthly, and its meetings will have a sense of urgency, warmth and excitement about them. It goes without saying that every elder should be in his or her place at the session meeting. Only solid excuses for absence like illness (serious illness!) are acceptable.

It has to be admitted that a fair number of elders, with, or more likely without, apology, regularly absent themselves and without apparent good reason. You can perhaps identify some of your fellow-elders who are in this position.

Some may do so because they do not like the way business is transacted in their session. They do not like conflict. Who can blame them if this is the case? Or it may be that they feel frustrated by decision-making that is rarely implemented. They do not like to have their time wasted.

For some elders the session meeting may be a dull affair, with a routine agenda repeated meeting after meeting. It may be that they are given no agenda to prepare for ahead of time and no minutes to keep track of progress.

It may be that virtually all the talking comes from the top table, assisted by Tom, Jim and Jeannie. The meeting may be structured in such a way as to shut out people who feel a bit nervous about speaking in a largish group.

Some of us are not as able as others to think fast on our feet. This does not mean that we cannot get to the point and make a useful contribution, but we need an environment that encourages our contribution.

Absence can be the consequence of poor management. When participation is not genuinely encouraged, some elders may feel that they have nothing to contribute and that they will not really be missed. The agenda may not be dull, but it seems so for them.

A *caring* session will do all it can to encourage participation and the sense of belonging. It will be less likely to suffer from unnecessary absenteeism.

Some elders absent themselves because they do not feel they belong at a deeper level. Years ago they were brought into the eldership on a light-weight contract, told there was little to it, and now, rightly or wrongly, they feel unable to fulfil the expectations of today. Something may have happened to them, shaking their faith in God, or self, or both.

Where this is the case we are faced with a real pastoral concern, one which we sometimes avoid, turn a blind eye towards, no doubt to the considerable pain of elders who no longer feel themselves to be elders.

A caring session will be aware of its members, including its absentees, and it will try to find ways of helping them.

May 1988

A cry from the heart

I HAVE been asked to respond to the question: 'How does an elder resign?' Is the question a cry from the heart? Is it asking for more than the answer: 'Have your session accept your resignation and your request to have your name removed from the ranks of the eldership?'

Perhaps underneath the question lie many feelings: of guilt about giving up something taken on for life; or fear of what other people might say, feel or do; of tiredness born of having been given too much to do in the life of a congregation; of personal inadequacy in pastoral visiting, or as a session seeks to deepen its lifestyle beyond what some elders were told the job meant when first approached.

Some would have us make the eldership a terminable appointment as in some other Presbyterian traditions. I resist any such move because I think of the vows of ordination to the eldership as akin to marriage vows and I would not advocate marriage vows which said—'I will love and cherish . . . for the next five years . . . with an option for a further five years if both parties agree'!

Better way

Marriage and the eldership, as I understand them, require a more long-term commitment. Though divorce is now rife, a bad thing for society, it is perhaps a good thing that the stigma attached to divorce, responsible for keeping many 'marriages' going, is lessening.

It is sad, however, when people, who once made to each other the promises of marriage, feel they have to seek divorce. It is especially so when it is made a bitter, acrimonious and graceless experience. But in some circumstances, despite the seriousness of the step, divorce may be the better way for the well-being of those concerned.

I think we can look at the eldership in the same way. If for whatever reason meaningful eldership is beyond repair, resignation may be the better way. If this is the case, may it be done gracefully and with the support and understanding of one's partners.

Perhaps breakdowns in both areas would be less if there had been better preparation for and more genuine support throughout the contract.

January 1987

Affirmation

TWO NEEDS of any human organisation, including a Christian one, are affirmation of its members and good lines of communication between its members.

I believe 'Session Matters' plays some part in meeting these needs for elders. Its existence and title certainly affirm the importance of session and the elders who form them.

The session is described in official documents as the 'lowest court' in the Kirk. To my mind, it is the most important court because it consists of the leaders of the basic unit of the Church since the birth of the Church to the present day—namely, the local congregation.

The Editor of *Life and Work* did a good thing when he introduced to the magazine the register of new elders. Session clerks can write in to have the names of their newly-ordained and inducted elders recorded in the pages of the Kirk's national magazine. I recommend that all of them do this. Newly-appointed elders deserve this recognition.

The eldership working party, which is now jointly led by Education Department and Ministry and Mission Department personnel, writes to every elder whose name appears in the register to express congratulations and to provide information and the offer of assistance. This offer includes the opportunity to join the new 'mailing to elders' service.

Presbytery

Communication, or the poverty of it, is a recognised problem in the Church. Elders for various reasons including their district work, should be aware of what is on offer to them and their members at the national level (courses and resources) and what Presbyteries are increasingly offering.

Returning to the matter of affirmation, I wonder whether it would not be a good thing to have the ordination of elders carried out at the Presbytery level, as it is for ministers.

This might help elders to see their place and role within the whole Church and not limited to their own congregations. The fact of their ordination could also be marked and celebrated by and in their own congregation.

It would be a good thing for a Presbytery to find ways of recognising and acknowledging, of affirming, the men and women within its bounds who have responded to the call to one of the most important offices within the Presbyterian Church—the elder-ship.

December 1988

Something to celebrate

ONE OF THE privileges of my ministry is to be able to travel the country, working with sessions and groups of elders. I often hear about good things that are being done and experienced—things which rarely receive any media coverage but which are heart-warming and encouraging.

On a course being run for ministers and session clerks, I was told about a good church social. It wasn't a dance, or a summer fair or a concert. It was in fact a party, held for an elder of 50 years ser-vice. It was a particularly happy occasion, a celebration of a person's half-century of devoted and valuable service in God's Church. We could do with more heart-warming, affirming occasions like that in the life of our congregations.

It was also a celebration of eldership. Even though I don't know the man, nor his session, I would like to have been present.

Good experience

Every morning when I come into my office I see a picture of the session to which I used to belong. I see the smiling faces of a team of men and women whose lives were so intertwined. The picture was taken on the day I was leaving them. I trust that was not the reason they were smiling so happily! I don't think it was. I think our faces showed the signs of celebration—of our being fellow-elders, of having shared so many personal joys and sorrows and difficulties, the challenge and responsibility of leading the ministry of God's people in that parish.

In Acts 20:17-38 you can read about another good experience of a group of elders. Before leaving Ephesus, Paul calls together the elders of the congregation. He shares with them what he feels about his life and ministry,

69

including his concern about the future. He feels he will not see them again and encourages them to look after their congregation and its witness to the Gospel. Before he leaves they pray together and their affection for each other is openly shown.

Of course our eldership is a responsibility, which can at times weigh heavily on us, but it is also a joy and privilege —something to celebrate.

January 1988

Whose responsibility?

THE QUESTION of responsibility is a crucial one for us as elders. It affects us collectively in our sessions, in our work of providing creative leadership for the ministry of our congregation. It affects us as individuals in the care we take of the people in our district.

We are ordained. God's seal is on us. We have the responsibility of doing our best for our God. Perhaps some of us seriously underestimate the weight and importance of our calling as elders. It is certainly true that some of us feel very weighed down by the

burden of our responsibility.

We can be trying to do our best to be an effective session but see little progress. We can be trying to do our best in our district work but see little return for our efforts.

'Yes, I'll be at Communion on Sunday.' 'Yes, I'll become more active in the life of the congregation.' Promises are made to us but often are not honoured.

We can feel taken for granted, put down. Of course there are times when we feel supported, appreciated and when promises made to us are honoured. When this is not the case, however, we can feel that somehow it is our fault. 'Where have we failed?' we ask ourselves.

Helpful maxim

When married to feelings of inadequacy and failure our responsibility as elders can become crushing.

I find the following maxim a help:

I am responsible for doing the best I can;

you are responsible for how you respond.

I find that to be a safeguard against apathy on my part. I am responsible for doing the best I can. It is also a safeguard against letting the attitudes of the apathetic in the congregation rule. As a session we will not offer this or that opportunity we believe in because people might not respond.

But we are not to carry the responsibility for the response others do or do not make. That is between them and God. That is their responsibility.

Take this column, for example. In the writing of it I try to be of service to my fellow-elders. That's my responsibility. As I travel the country, many of you say you find it of value and I am glad, but what you do with it is your responsibility.

As elders we have enough to do to carry out responsibility without also carrying the responsibility of others.

July 1985

Feeling inadequate?

SOME TIME ago I was greatly saddened—not for him, but for those of us who loved him—by the sudden and unexpected death of an elder who had been a friend and fellow-worker. We had spent many a youth weekend together, shared many a pastoral concern and worked well together in the leadership of our congregation.

Though highly respected by his fellow elders, by the folks in his district and by the young people he served as a youth leader, Alex often felt inadequate to be an elder. He was anything but.

An elder with a district to care for has a great calling. Real pastoral concern takes time, sensitivity, devotion, freely given year in and year out. Such devotion is not always appreciated. It can be taken for granted. Sometimes it has to face put-downs and discouragements —the homes that refuse entry; the complaints and excuses that are made over and over again; the promises often made but never kept. Such responses invite us to blame ourselves, feel a failure, feel inadequate.

In my experience many a fine elder and effective Christian feels inadequate. And what is true of an individual elder can also be true of a session. When as a session we are trying to give real, creative leadership to our congregation, and meeting with little response; when we are trying to provide opportunities for worship, support, learning, service and meeting with great indifference—we can feel so very inadequate.

Regarding our feelings, it is useful to remember that we choose how we feel. People can invite us to feel good or bad, but

71

it is we who decide what we are going to feel. We have the power to decide how we are to respond to discouragement.

It is also useful to keep in mind that it is our responsibility (individually and collectively) to offer the best we can; it is other people's responsibility what they do with our offer. This I find a great safeguard against letting apathy rule. We have to offer the best we can. It is also a safeguard against carrying the burden of other people's responsibility. If we are sincerely doing what we can for God and his people, that is all God expects of us. How others respond is between them and God. That is not our burden.

Doing our best is, of course, not easy. It is costly. Eldership is no light-weight responsibility. When I feel inadequate I find real comfort and strength in the recognition that so many of the leaders of God's people in the Bible were clearly flawed people, people inadequate in many ways, but people through whom God could achieve much. What He did with them, he can do with us.

March 1985

The matchstick problem

LET ME share three memories with you.

As a boy I remember the parties my parents had with their friends. This was back in the pre-TV days of music-making and party games. The house rang with laughter.

Often they would play cards, playing not for money but for matchsticks. I used to watch my father risk a match on every hand, and I watched him slowly but steadily always lose his supply of matches. I learned a lesson. He who invests little is unlikely to get much in the way of a return and may lose even what he has.

I share this memory to focus attention on a problem that faces the Church. It is the 'matchstick' problem—a low level of commitment; an investment rate which brings little or no return to the cause, or to the individual for that matter.

As a teenager I remember toiling away unaided as a raw Sunday school teacher amidst a number of other teenagers who similarly toiled. The older teachers would turn up on the Sunday to teach. No doubt they did their own lesson preparation. They were not prepared, however, to invest time for a shared preparation class. Eventually we young people met together to pool our inexperience and to try to help each other. We found the extra investment worthwhile.

A good return

As elders are we investing enough to enable the great cause we are engaged in to move forwards?

Are we personally getting a good return on our investment in the sense of the joy of our calling, the feeling of maturing in our faith and spirituality, and of being of real value to our Lord and His people?

We are the leaders of our congregations. Would more investment in prayer and Bible study yield a good return?

Most of us are involved in pastoral concern, which, if not studiously maintained at a 'matchstick' level, involves us in a whole range of human problems. Would investment in some kind of learning programme be helpful? Would it help if your session provided opportunities to share experience and to support one another in this regard?

A third memory is of four Sunday school teachers who asked for a course of study which would take them beyond what they were teaching to their children. This extra investment on their part led to an education programme for all the Sunday school staff, and in due course to a wide range of opportunities for the whole congregation under the leadership of the session.

October 1983

'Wishing or willing'

IT SEEMS to me that many members of the Church and, perhaps, many of us who are elders, are suffering a lack of confidence—in our faith and in the enabling power of God. If this is so, it is not surprising given, amongst other things:

The indifference so many people around us have regarding the Church;

The difficulties many people have, Church members as well as non-Church people, regarding the Bible and various Christian beliefs;

The lack of serious adult learning opportunities in the life of many congregations.

A lack of confidence on the part of some elders may also have something to do with the growing awareness that district work is about caring for people, something not to be confused with the delivering of Communion cards.

It may be further compounded by the growing appreciation of the complexity of the leadership role of the session.

Clearly the Church is no longer an institution to which most people belong. Many of our own children, though not necessarily hostile to the Church, have no active part in it. Christians in our land are once again in a missionary situation.

Faced with this we can, as individuals and as sessions, throw in the towel or we can sit in the corner of the ring and lament the situation.

We may sincerely *wish* the situation were different, but do not *will* it to be different. Often *wishing* waits for someone else to do this or that. *Willing* is more likely to take an active part in changing a situation. Our Christian faith is about the latter.

We have the resources. Think of the potential that exists in our nationwide network of congregations and sessions, each with its own minister, and backed up by the Kirk's small but energetic band of full-time field staff, and the growing network of voluntary, Presbytery-based resource people. We can use these people if we have a *will* to.

There are resource materials and learning opportunities, perhaps more than every before, which we can find out about and use—if we have a *will* to.

These resources, co-operating with God through living prayerfully and worshipping and learning together, will change the situation. If you feel like doing a bit of lamenting, ask yourself who would have bet a first century AD halfpenny on Christianity becoming a world-wide religion, and the Christian Church being very much alive, world-wide, 2000 years later?

December 1989

LEADING GOD'S PEOPLE

*What are Church Elders for? What is the job of a
Session in the modern Church?*
This book provides some baseline thinking
about the Eldership. It applies the key ideas of
teamwork and leadership to the Session. It looks
at some common problems, how to manage the
Session team, and how to gain ground.

Elders, and others engaged in Christian
leadership, are encouraged not only to read
this book as a text, but also to use it as the
basis for individual activity and group discussion.

It aims to make a contribution towards
realising the vast potential of the Eldership in
today's Church—in enabling and directing
God's people.

CARING FOR GOD'S PEOPLE

How do we care for God's people?
Elders are entrusted with the care of a
district, or a number of members in their
congregation, in the Presbyterian tradition
of the Church. Sometimes they can be
called upon to exercise a concern for non-
Church members as well.

For this important and demanding responsibility of caring for people, Elders are
rarely given the correct training or the vital
support they need and deserve for such work.

This book is designed to provide guidance
for the individual Elder, to facilitate training
opportunities and encourage mutual support.

THE SAINT ANDREW PRESS
EDINBURGH

The 'Session Matters' column by Stewart Matthew is one of the many contributions to the Kirk's life and vigour by LIFE AND WORK, The Record of the Church of Scotland. Published monthly, this magazine provides a news service, a means of Christian teaching in print, and a forum for the people of the Church.

Some of its articles and letters are controversial and much publicised in the media. Other features, like 'Session Matters', have regularly met the needs of different groups in the Church, and have been quietly but profoundly appreciated.

Though mainly circulated through congregations, LIFE AND WORK also has postal subscribers thoughout the world. For details and subscription rates (air-mail quotations on request) contact:

LIFE AND WORK
121 George Street, Edinburgh EH2 4YN